1986

Adoption and Race

Child Care Policy and Practice

General Editor: Tony Hall, Director and Secretary,
British Agencies for Adoption & Fostering

In preparation:

Specialist Fostering
Tony Hipgrave and Martin Shaw

Children in Care Revisited
Pamela Mann

ADOPTION AND RACE

Black, Asian and mixed race children in white families

OWEN GILL and BARBARA JACKSON

Batsford Academic and Educational Ltd
St. Martin's Press, Inc.

in association with

British Agencies for Adoption & Fostering

First published 1983

Typeset by Colset Pte Ltd, Singapore
and printed in Great Britain by
Billing & Son Ltd
Worcester
for the publishers
Batsford Academic and Educational Ltd
4 Fitzhardinge Street
London W1H 0AH
and St. Martin's Press Inc.,
175 Fifth Avenue, New York, NY10010

ISBN 0 7134 20235 (UK)

Library of Congress Cataloging in Publication Data

Gill, Owen.
    Adoption and race.

    Bibliography: p.
    1. Interracial adoption – United States – Case studies.
2. Race awareness in children – Case studies.   3. Inter –
racial adoption – Great Britain – Case studies.
4. Adoptees – United States – Family relationships – Case
studies.   5. Adoptees – Great Britain – Family relation –
ships – Case studies   I. Jackson, Barbara.   II. Title.
HV875.G586 1983   362.7'34   82-42714
ISBN 0-312-00495-8

CONTENTS

List of Tables

Acknowledgements

This project was funded by the Small Grants Committee of the Department of Health and Social Security, and we would like to thank the Committee and its members for their support.

We are grateful for the help we received during the course of the research from a number of colleagues. Sarah Malone played an important part in the planning and pilot-interview stages of the research and also conducted half of the main interviews. Daphne Holbrook gave us valuable help in the design of the interview schedule and has also generously given us permission to refer in the report to her unpublished work. We are also grateful to Olwen Rowlands, who helped us considerably in planning the interviews, and to Mary Hellard and Elva Makin who found families for us to interview at the pilot stage. Daphne Johnstone transcribed the interview tapes and typed the drafts of the report with great precision and speed. Tony Hall gave us good-humoured support and valuable advice throughout the project.

But our main debt of gratitude is to the parents and children we talked to. They welcomed us into their homes, gave generously of their time, and allowed us to share in their family experiences. We sincerely thank them all.

Owen Gill
Barbara Jackson

February 1982

1

Transracial adoption

The term *transracial adoption* refers to children being adopted by parents of a different racial origin to their own. In the overwhelming majority of cases this means white parents adopting black or mixed-race children. The research presented in this book is an examination of the outcome of such adoptions. It has been carried out at a time when not only are there very significant changes in the nature of adoption in this country, but also when a large questionmark hangs over transracial adoption itself. Many people argue that children adopted in this way will suffer problems of 'identity'. Others argue that such adoptions represent the exploitation of the black community by white society: blacks have become a 'donor' group of children for whites.

In this introductory chapter we discuss the development of transracial adoption in the United States and Britain and then examine in more detail some of the criticisms.

Transracial adoption in the United States

No accurate figures exist for the number of transracial adoptions made in the United States, but Simon and Altstein, writing in 1975, estimated that since 1961 approximately 15,000 children had been transracially adopted in that country.[1] This figure includes inter-country adoptions as well as the adoption of those children whose natural parents were resident in the United States. Reviewing the history of transracial adoption in the United States, Simon and Altstein wrote that it

> began in the late 1940s. It gained momentum in the mid-1950s. It diminished during the early 1960s, rose again in the mid-1960s, and waned in the early 1970s . . . . Most of the social forces that define white — non-white relationships are evident in the development of transracial adoption, from white paternalism, through the civil rights movement, and culminating in a militant awareness of non-white racial minorities of their social, economic and political influence.[2]

They claimed that by 1975 transracial adoption of American and Indian children by white parents was almost at an end; the numbers were 'so small as to be insignificant'.[3]

1

There were two interconnected reasons for this dramatic decline. The first was that agencies were realising that finding adoptive parents from the black community was possible and, second, there was a consistent attack on the practice of transracial adoption from black welfare groups and others. At its 1972 conference, the National Association of Black Social Workers expressed 'vehement opposition' to the practice of placing black children with white families. They committed themselves to fight against transracial adoption and condemned it as a form of 'genocide' in which the black community's most valuable resource — its children — was being taken from it to satisfy the needs of childless white couples.

At the same time other voices were being raised against transracial adoption. For instance, Jones questioned the ability of white parents, no matter how deeply imbued with goodwill, to grasp the totality of the problem of being black in a white society and to create in the child a sense of black identity.[4] And in a much-quoted article Chestang asked:

> Can white families assure black children an environment in which there is optimal opportunity for growth, development and indentification?[5]

And already by 1973 the Child Welfare League of America had changed its guidelines or 'standards' on racial background in relation to adoption, stating that

> it is preferable to place children in families of their own racial background.

One of the reasons for this was that

> children placed in adoptive families with similar racial characteristics can become more easily integrated into the average family group and community.[6]

Transracial adoption in Britain

It is impossible to gauge the exact number of children who have been adopted transracially in this country, but the available evidence suggests that transracial adoptions became numerically significant later than in the United States. With the decrease in the number of available white babies, the number of transracial placements would seem to have grown from the mid-1960s and increased further during the early to mid-1970s. Indeed, one of the central criticisms related to transracial adoption is that it was only when the supply of healthy white babies for adoption had failed that black babies were seen to be suitable for adoption by white couples. In other words, adoption agencies saw their central purpose as being to provide children for childless white couples rather than to regard the needs of the children as paramount.

Although black and mixed-race children were increasingly placed for adoption, there was a failure to recruit adoptive parents from the black community in this country.[7] The reasons for this are beyond the scope of the present study, but it is argued that the cultural bias of white-orientated adoption agencies and workers, the unwillingness of black parents to submit themselves to the investigations of a white bureaucracy and the alien nature of formal adoption arrangements to the West Indian and Asian community are all significant. Added to this, and compared with the United States, Britain has a proportionately smaller black community and does not have an established black middle class — and adoption, at least historically, has been primarily a middle-class preserve.

The position in this country now appears to be similar in many ways to that in the United States a decade ago. Strong claims are being made that wherever possible black and mixed-race children should be placed with parents of their own racial background. For instance, Fitzgerald writes:

The first question to ask about black children waiting for a permanent substitute family is, should the aim be to place the child with a family of the same racial origin? In my view the answer is emphatically yes.[8]

This view is echoed by James:

Greater understanding and recognition of the needs of black children and increased pressure from the ethnic minority communities have raised questions about transracial placements and led to increased emphasis being placed upon the recruitment of black families.[9]

Although this may be a view that is expressed increasingly, there is no clear evidence that it has been matched by significant changes in practice. In the course of our research we contacted 30 adoption workers involved in the placement of black children in 17 agencies. The picture that emerges is that although some successes are being achieved in finding black homes for black children, the most likely placement for these children is still with white families.

The majority of workers appear to accept the desirability of finding black homes for black children and yet in practice such placements do not occur. All but a few of the workers we contacted said that they had difficulty in recruiting enough 'suitable' black families for their waiting black children. Some of the workers told us that although it might be felt that a same-race placement was ideal for a particular child, the likely delay in finding such a placement was often a key factor in the decision to place with a white family.

3

Others told us that financial restrictions limit their ability to launch recruitment campaigns to find suitable black families when numerous white couples are waiting for similar children. For a variety of reasons, therefore, transracial placements are still, if a little guiltily, being made.

The arguments against transracial adoption

From this brief review it is clear that transracial adoption, in both the United States and Britain, is a controversial area of child-care policy. Before embarking on the results of our study, therefore, it is necessary to clarify the arguments against transracial adoption. Such clarity is not always apparent in the statements of its critics. Broadly speaking there are two categories of potential criticism:

1 Criticisms based on discrimination against the black community
2 Criticisms based on the anticipated experiences of a black child in a white family

In the first category are criticisms based on the relations between the black and white communities in contemporary society, which see transracial adoption representing in microcosm the oppression of black people in white society. These include:

— Blacks have always serviced whites. Now they are servicing them in the ultimate fashion, by providing them with children.[10]
— Transracial adoption takes from the black community its most valuable resource which is its children.
— The black community cannot hope to maintain its pride and dignity if advantage is defined as being brought up by white families.

These are arguments related to the position of black people in white society. There are of course alternative arguments, such as the benefits to integration to be derived from transracial adoption and the argument, expressed by one black father of an adopted black child interviewed in the course of our own research, that to have policies against transracial adoption is a form of apartheid. Nevertheless, it is the ideological arguments *against* transracial adoption which have been put forward most strongly in the United States and this country.

The second category of criticisms, those based on the anticipated experience of a black child in a white family, includes the following:

— Because of the child's obvious difference of racial and physical background the parents and other members of the family will come to see the

child as 'not belonging to this family'. Close and intimate family relations will not develop between the child and other family members.
— Because of obvious differences of racial and physical background the child will have a self-perception of 'not belonging to this family'. The result of this will be a deep sense of personal isolation.
— Because the child is adopted by white parents contact outside the home is primarily white. Although over time, racial background may be insignificant in the family, it will continue to be crucially significant outside the family. The child will be unable to relate effectively in the outside world and will retreat into the family world.
— Identity confusion. Children placed transracially will come to face major problems of who they are, black or white. The confusion will be experienced as so central that they will have a poor self-concept and low self-esteem.
— Because the children are black, but growing up in white families, they will not be taught the necessary coping mechanisms for dealing with the hostility and rejection of white society. These coping mechanisms can only be taught in the black family.
— Because of being brought up in white families, transracially adopted children will not be able to relate to members of the black community. They will be rejected not only by the white community, but also by the black community.

It is necessary to make the distinction between these two categories of criticism because 'experiential' arguments are often confused with 'black community' arguments and each category demands a different form of research inquiry.

It is not our intention at this stage to become involved in the 'black community' arguments, although we shall return to them later in the book when we come to balance the findings of our study against the wider policy issues. We would, however, take it as self-evident that the one-way traffic of black or mixed-race children from the black to the white community indicates the relative power and position of the different ethnic groups in British society.

However, such a position should not detract from research into the experiences of those families which have been created by transracial adoption. Unless there is a radical change in the effectiveness of welfare agencies in recruiting black adopters, or unless alternative families cease to be needed for black or mixed-race children, a proportion of such children will, at least for the foreseeable future, continue to be placed in white homes.

5

Previous research

It is helpful briefly to discuss the findings of previous research studies in this field. In doing this it should, however, be stressed that almost all of these findings are based on the experiences of families with young or very young children and that in most of the studies the children themselves were not active participants in the research.

The first major investigation of transracially-adopted children in the United States was the work of Fanshel.[11] Fanshel conducted annual interviews for five years with the adoptive white families of nearly a hundred children of Indian background. After rating the children's overall adjustment he concluded that more than 50 per cent of the children were performing 'extremely well' in all spheres of life and another 25 per cent were performing in a way that made the outlook for their future adjustment 'very hopeful'. Only 10 per cent of the children appeared to be experiencing difficulties which made the prognosis of likely outcome uncertain.

In 1974 Grow and Shapiro published the results of a study of 125 transracially-adopted children with a median age of 8.8 years.[12] Most were described as doing average or above average work in class and being in good health. They were described as getting along well with other children, having close friends and good relationships with siblings. The children compared well on the total personality adjustment scores with a sample of white adopted children using similar evaluation instruments. The majority of parents in the study described their experience in rearing the study child as satisfying and felt that the adoption had turned out well or better than they expected. Using a variety of measures, Grow and Shapiro judged 77 per cent of their sample to represent successful adoptions. This, they concluded, compared favourably with the results obtained in studies of adoptions by white families of white children. Although the Grow and Shapiro study provided strong evidence for the successful general development of the children it studied, it has been criticised by Chimezie for not attempting to investigate the question of the child's sense of racial identity.[13]

Simon and Altstein investigated this aspect of transracial adoption in a study published in 1977.[14] The children studied by Simon and Altstein were considerably younger than in the earlier study, ranging from three years to eight years, with an average age of slightly over four years. The research design was similar to that used in earlier studies of racial identity and awareness in black children in which the child was shown dolls of different colours and was asked to indicate the doll that 'looks like you', 'looks bad', is a 'nice colour', and other questions designed to indicate actual and ideal identities.

The researchers could find no significant preference for the white dolls among the transracially-adopted children. Simon and Altstein concluded:

the unusual family environment in which these children are being reared may result in their acquiring deviant racial attitudes and in their not sharing with other American children a sense that white is preferable to other races.[15]

Recently Simon and Altstein have published the results of a follow-up survey of their original sample.[16] The average age of the children at the time of the follow-up was eleven years. Of the original 204 families, 133 replied to a postal questionnaire. Altogether 25 sets of parents described problems related to the adoption and/or to the racial difference between themselves and their adopted children. Simon and Altstein concluded that this compared favourably with other studies of white adopted children.

In this follow-up they also asked the parents how the children identified themselves. Fifty-four per cent of the parents said their children identified as Black American, Indian or Korean, 28 per cent said their children had a 'mixed' identity, 15 per cent said their children identified as white. The remaining three per cent did not know. But the children themselves were not approached and the validity of asking parents to answer for their children's racial identity is of course open to question.

The only American study that appears to have directly tackled the issue of the identity of transracially-adopted children in adolescence is the work of Kim[17] who used a sample of 406 Korean children adopted in the United States. Their ages ranged from 12 to 17 at the time of the research. Kim used a postal survey to administer the Tennessee Self-Concept Scale and a scale designed to measure adolescent socialisation. On the basis of responses he concluded that the young people investigated had little 'Korean' identity, but had developed healthy self-concepts relative to other groups of adolescents. He also concluded that family environment factors were positively related to self-concept.

In this country the amount of research into transracial adoption has been very limited. The most detailed research has been the two follow-ups of the British Adoption Project (BAP).[18] The BAP was initiated in the mid-1960s to answer the question, 'Can families be found for coloured children?' This now seems a strange question in the light of present-day experience when children with severe mental, physical and emotional difficulties are being adopted, but when the BAP was conceived, racial background was considered a major handicap to placement. As a result of the project, homes for 53 black or mixed-race children were found with 51 couples. A majority, but not all of this group, were families in which both parents were white and the child was either black or mixed-race.

In 1969, at the end of the original four-year project, each of the BAP families was assessed.[19] This assessment was necessarily limited in scope because of the age of the children and the comparatively short length of time since their adoption. The interview covered health, development, personality, social and family relationships and problems attributable to the child's racial background and adoptive status. A series of group discussions was also held, involving 50 of the couples.

Each child and family was rated separately by Lois Raynor on the basis of the interview and all that was known about the family. An independent rating was also made. In general, the children and families seemed to be making satisfactory adjustment and progress. According to both sets of ratings 94 per cent of the children were said to have made a very good or satisfactory adjustment. There was some discrepancy in the ratings of the parents, but both assessed that more than 75 per cent were making a very good or satisfactory adjustment as adoptive parents. Both sets of ratings resulted in only three children and two families causing significant concern.

In the group discussions, parents related, almost without exception, that their child had been a centre of attraction among strangers, but generally the incidents were minor and apparently not of sufficient seriousness for them to question the adoption or to seek outside help. The group discussions also highlighted some confusion among the parents about the likely inherited characteristics of their children.

The next part of the BAP follow-up (1974–1975)[20] took place after the children had all entered school and they had all been told about their adoption. Once again, interviews were sought with each of the couples and 49 of the 51 families participated. The majority of the parents were also involved in small group discussions. Four of the BAP couples had divorced or separated. In each case the child remained with the adoptive mother.

Once again, each family and child was given a separate rating. Among the factors which were taken into consideration were the parents' level of satisfaction with the adoption, their expressed anxiety over the child's background and discussing her adoptive status with her, their perception of the child, and the degree of cohesion in the marriage and in the home.

In general, the findings confirmed those of the previous follow-up. Four of the children were described as giving cause for concern. Although those with problems showed a slight increase from the previous follow-up, the 'success rate' was still in keeping with the comparable studies done by

Seglow, Pringle and Wedge[21] in this country and by Grow and Shapiro[22] and Fanshel[23] in America.

By this stage the BAP parents had all formulated a policy related to dealing with their child's racial background. In 11 of the families no emphasis was placed on the child's cultural or racial origins. This seemed to be a positive stance to raise the child as an English/white child. Twenty-two of the couples stated that they thought it was important for the child to feel pride in racial background, but felt that the initiative for this should come from the child. If the child had shown no interest or had not responded to tentative approaches made by the parents, they felt it wrong to press. The remaining 16 couples described varying degrees of encouragement to their children to be interested in and proud of their origins.

Apart from earlier reports of the follow-ups to the British Adoption Project, the only significant British research appears to be that of Bagley and Young[24] who followed up a group of 27 mixed-race children and three black children who had been adopted by white parents and whose average age was 7.3 years. Their development was compared with that of three other groups: (a) 24 mixed-race children in the care of the local authority; (b) 30 adopted white children and (c) 30 randomly-chosen white children attending the same classes as the sample group and of the same age. The study found that the transracially-adopted group had excellent comparative levels of adjustment. In terms of racial identity just under half of the mixed-race children adopted by white parents identified themselves as white. The research also suggested a positive relationship between the adoptive parents being 'racially aware' and the children having a lower level of negative stereotypes of black figures.

The results of the Bagley and Young research are important, but again it must be stressed that this research, as the other research referred to, was conducted on children who were considerably younger than the age at which the difficulties of transracial adoption are typically presumed to occur.

The present research

The research presented in this book is the third follow-up of the BAP. Our research task was to examine the outcome of these adoptions already referred to. More specifically, our purpose was to examine the experiences of this group of families and their adopted children when, if criticisms have been well-founded, the difficulties would have become evident. Also, crucially, the research was planned for a time when the children themselves could discuss their experiences, feelings, identifications and anticipations. Lois

9

Raynor, reporting in 1970 on the placements and very early years of the BAP children, wrote:

> It is not known whether the strains and stress of adolescence will be very much greater for non-white children in English families than for children growing up in an adoptive family of their own race.[25]

It is to this question that this study directly addresses itself. We do this by presenting the detailed experiences of the BAP families which have been created in this way. By using wherever possible the words of the parents and children and by attempting to enter into their worlds, we have attempted to throw some light on the anticipated difficulties of transracial adoption. In doing so we were in the unique and fortunate position not only of knowing a great deal about the characteristics of the original placements and their development over more than a decade, but also of having a very high response-rate from the original BAP families (see Chapter 2).

Synopsis

In Chapter 2 we discuss the methodological issues that have arisen in carrying out the research and describe our approach to interviewing the parents and children.

Chapter 3 contains background details on the 36 families and children who form the basis of the study, and in Chapter 4 we examine the relationships inside the family from the perspective of the children and their parents.

Chapter 5 focuses upon the relationships that the child has outside the family and evaluates the children's progress at school. This is done on the basis of the parents' and children's interviews and also on questionnaires completed by the schools.

In Chapter 6 we turn directly to the issue of racial background and examine the contact that the families have with the black community and the parents' policies about the racial identity of their children.

Chapter 7 is concerned with the children's beliefs, knowledge and self-concepts in relation to their racial background, and in Chapter 8 we examine whether the children have experienced the anticipated difficulties of being black in a white family.

In Chapter 9 we explore the way in which adoption has been dealt with in the families, and examine the children's knowledge of their natural parents and their current desire for knowledge.

For comparative purposes, Chapter 10 looks at eight families of the original BAP group who had not adopted transracially (e.g., either one or both adoptive parents were black).

Finally, in Chapter 11, we bring together the findings of the study and then put them into the context of wider policy issues.

A note on terminology

A number of issues of terminology have arisen in writing the report. First, we have faced a problem over the collective word to use to describe the subjects of the study, who are now aged 13–15. To be constantly referring to 'teenagers' or 'adolescents' has seemed ponderous and with obvious misgivings we have continued to refer to them as 'children'. Second, as more than half of the study children are girls, when we discuss the transracially-adopted child in general we refer to 'she' and 'her' rather than to 'he' and 'his'. More important, the third problem that conducting and writing up this research has presented us with is whether we should refer to the children as 'black' or 'coloured' or use another description. We shall return to the research implications of this in the next chapter. But at this stage it is necessary to say that we use the term 'black' throughout this report in preference to others because it signifies the dignity of the black community — a dignity which the debate on transracial adoption has to recognise. The use of the term 'black' also nicely marks the passage of time from the 1960s when the BAP set out to find homes for 'coloured' or 'non-white' children.

Also we are aware that we have used the term 'black' as a shorthand way of referring to children who are often distinguished as 'black, Asian or mixed-race children'. We have obviously done this with misgivings, but are aware that no single terminology will be acceptable to everyone.

2

Talking to the parents and children: research methodology

A variety of methods was used to look at the experiences of the BAP families and children. We conducted separate semi-structured interviews with both parents and children; we asked parents to complete standardised questionnaires on their children's health and social adjustment; and we asked the children to fill in standardised questionnaires to assess their self-esteem. We also, with the parents' permission, contacted the study children's schools and asked the teachers most involved with them to complete a short questionnaire on their progress and experience at school.

Despite this variety, the main data presented in this book are the tape-recorded words of the parents and children, and it is the issues surrounding this method on which we concentrate in this chapter. Methodological issues are, however, never very far from the surface in the study and we return to them in relation to specific approaches at appropriate points in the book.

Pilot interviews

Before interviewing the BAP parents and children, we carried out a series of pilot interviews. It proved difficult to find suitable families, but eventually, through the help of a social services department and a local 'Parent to Parent Information on Adoption Service' (PPIAS) group, we were able to contact 12 families with transracially-adopted children of similar ages to the BAP group. Several of the children we talked to were, however, under 12 and one boy was aged 16.

The pilot interviews helped us to formulate the questions and the approach for interviewing the children. Most importantly, they made us optimistic that, approached in a sensitive way, the children in the main study would be prepared to talk about both their adoption and about issues relating to their different racial background. In particular, they taught us that if we were prepared to be interested in the children for themselves and see adoption and racial background as simply one feature of their lives, then they would be forthcoming on these issues.

Because of the sensitivity of the issues concerned we also made a point of contacting a number of the pilot parents after the visits to see if there had been any adverse or unhappy reaction on the part of the children to our visits. We were encouraged to find that there appeared to have been no such difficulties.

Talking about racial background

The study highlighted a number of methodological issues. The first was one of *design*. In talking to the children it was necessary to have a degree of standardised structure to the interview. Yet in structuring the interview we ran the risk that aspects of family life and experience would appear more important than they perhaps were. This is particularly the case with racial background. Obviously, we had to ask questions that attempted to obtain information on how racial background is perceived, dealt with and experienced, but we did not want either to give undue emphasis to racial background or to emphasise the differences between parent and child.

In terms of interviewing the children the main challenge we faced, therefore, was to develop an interview schedule that would allow the children to be forthcoming about their experiences and feelings and at the same time allow them to put their own meanings and interpretations onto their social world. We followed the approach advocated by Kitwood, whose research

> did not deal with adolescents' answers to hypothetical questions, but with values developed in facing the realities of everyday life where there is great (and methodologically inconvenient) variety.[1]

Of particular value to us in planning the interviews was Kitwood's development and use of the 'situations grid'. The adolescent respondent is asked to describe situations in which, for instance, 'you were very angry or annoyed', 'you got on really well with people' or 'you felt you were powerless or misunderstood'. In using this approach for his study of adolescent values, Kitwood found that

> the 'situations' seemed to provide a natural access to the participants' central concerns, and to be stimulating a kind of personal and expressive narrative that we had not encountered from adolescents.[2]

We were able to use this approach fruitfully and to modify it for our particular purposes. It enabled us to get at the general character of the children's everyday lives, and to analyse responses in terms of the significance that the children themselves attached to their different racial background. Questions such as 'describe a time when you felt alone because of

13

your colour' were used to get the children to describe their feelings and experience directly related to race (see Chapter 9).

The second general problem was related to *vocabulary*. When we were designing the interview schedule we attempted to find an appropriate vocabulary in which to ask parents and children about race. The term 'non-white' which was used in the original report was clearly no longer appropriate. As was pointed out by one of the fathers in the pilot interviews, it defined the children by what they were not rather than by what they were. The pilot interviews also gave us the opportunity to experiment with terms like 'black', 'coloured' and 'brown', but none of these proved appropriate for all families. Eventually, we realised that it was impossible to find terms which were both neutral and universally acceptable. As a result, early in the eventual parents' interview, we asked a question about the vocabulary in use in the family and were able to use this in presenting later questions. The lessons of this are twofold. To interview people it is necessary to use a vocabulary which is consistent with their own. Also, the vocabulary in use in our families is data in its own right. The words used to describe racial background offer us valuable insights into the way in which racial background is being defined by the families and the children (see Chapter 7).

The third general problem we faced is one often referred to in studies of racial issues; the racial background of the researchers. Although far from conclusive, there is some evidence that the racial background of the interviewer can play a part in determining responses. After a review of the literature Brah, Fuller, Louden and Miles tentatively concluded that

> with regard to ethnic identification and preference studies ... the evidence suggests *on balance* that the respondents' responses may be influenced in the direction of greater favourability towards the racial group to which the investigator belongs.[3]

However, it follows from this conclusion that just as white interviewers can affect the responses of black children, so also can black interviewers affect their responses in the opposite way. Also, this research gives us only limited guidelines for examining transracial adoption because it is concerned with children living with their own racial group. In the event both the interviewers in our study were white. It is impossible to justify this decision with certainty, but we would support it on the basis that these children, as will be demonstrated, were living in an almost entirely white world. Many were not used to black people in their everyday lives. Also, as will be apparent later, we could detect no reluctance on the part of the children to talk about their racial background.

14

Mixed-race children

Another issue we have had to contend with both in planning and under-taking the research, and in writing this book, has been that a significant proportion of the study children have mixed racial origins in the sense that one of their natural parents is white and the other is black (see Chapter 3). It is sometimes argued that the mixed-race child is a black child because this is how society will see and respond to her. It would have made our research task more straightforward to have accepted this definition and to have regarded the children as an homogeneous group. However, although this might well be the way that society regards such children, it may not be the way that the children perceive themselves,[4] or how their parents see them. It is possible, particularly in the case of transracial adoptions, that parents and mixed-race children will choose to concentrate on their whiteness rather than their blackness.

We have tackled this problem by distinguishing the black and mixed-race children in the general discussion where responses seem significantly different. In addition, specific reference is made to the two groups in our discussion of racial identity (see Chapters 6 and 7).

Interviewing the BAP families

The interviewing of the main group of families was carried out between November 1980 and May 1981.[5] Each family was visited by one of the inter-viewers, who talked separately to both the parents and the child. The average length of the parents' interview was just over one and a half hours; the longest was nearly three hours, the shortest, thirty minutes. The average length of the children's interviews was just over one hour, ranging from two hours to thirty minutes. The visits to the family were therefore often lengthy. Most were carried out at weekends and it was usual for the inter-viewer to arrive at midday and to leave in the early evening.

In this section we describe briefly some of the practical issues that we faced in carrying out these interviews. The first and most important point was that we had to be aware that we were dealing with two potentially highly sensi-tive issues — adoption and racial background. The approach of the inter-viewers was crucial in determining the level of experience that the parents and children were prepared to share. Also, as the interviews were to show, it was possible that even in these families the issues of adoption and racial background were only rarely discussed. So, in effect, by asking for permission to interview the children, we were asking for permission to raise these subjects in the family. We had in the interview schedule a question

15

which asked the parents when was the last time that they had discussed the child's racial background with her. A number of the parents said that they only rarely discussed it, but had in fact done so in anticipation of our visit.

Further evidence for the necessity of a sensitive approach came from some parents who described their feelings at our coming to interview them. One mother said she had initially resented the interviewer making contact because it had 'reminded' her that her child was adopted.

With the parents there was also a danger that by coming to interview them on their approach to bringing up a child of a different racial background we were implying that they ought to have definite policies on this and that there was perhaps a specific professionally-accepted approach. This echoes the earlier point that in constructing an interview schedule the researcher is implying a certain stance and perception of reality which the research subjects may or may not share.

The pattern of interviews was kept as consistent as possible for the whole group. After arrival we aimed to speak to the parents and the child together, explaining the purpose of the visit. This served not only to tell the child what the visit was about, but also to validate us in the children's eyes because we were talking about the purpose in front of their parents. In those few initial interviews where we did not follow this principle, we had the feeling that whilst we talked to the parents, the children were left in something of a vacuum, realising that their parents were talking about them, but without knowing where they fitted in.

In almost all of the families we talked to the parents before the children and this worked well. It allowed background information to be obtained about the child, and the parents could advise the interviewer of areas of the child's life which were particularly sensitive. These arguments in our experience outweigh alternative arguments that by interviewing the child first, she sees herself as the focus of interest rather than an appendage to her parents.

In several interviews we did, however, have to talk to the child first because one of the parents had not yet arrived. The experience of these interviews confirmed us in our approach of talking to parents first. In one interview the interviewer carried out the whole interview underneath a photograph of the natural mother. The child did not say who this was and the interviewer had no way of telling. Later, in talking to the parents they told the story of how they had come by the photograph and its significance to the child. Such background knowledge and opportunity for talking fully about the natural mother would have been useful in talking to the child. In another case where the child was interviewed first, there was a potentially disastrous moment at the beginning of the interview when the interviewer said that there would be some questions about the fact that the child's first father was Indian. The girl replied, 'Is he? I didn't know that.' It became apparent later that the child was aware that her first father was Indian and that perhaps she was doing a little testing out. But it created the kind of experience that the interviewer would prefer not to go through again!

After we had talked to the parents we asked their permission to talk to the children, a question that had been first raised when we had contacted them by telephone some weeks earlier. Generally, the parents were happy for us to do this. Where necessary we described in a little more detail the form the children's interview would take and showed them the interview schedule. This is a further argument for talking to parents first. It allowed a rapport to build up between parents and interviewer, and the parents to develop confidence in the way in which the interviewer was likely to approach their child. In the event, the parents of only three children were a little hesitant about giving permission for the interview, and none refused.

Some of the interviews with the children took place in family living-rooms or kitchens, but a number took place in their bedrooms. This was often suggested by the parents as a way of getting away from the general mêlée of family life and also so that the child could talk to us on her own 'territory'. Most of the children seemed to enjoy answering the questions and for several of the children we were left with the impression that it had offered them an unusual opportunity to talk to an adult and be the sole focus of attention. Only one of the children we talked to seemed to be uneasy about the interview and she asked us not to contact her for the next follow-up of the group in five years' time. Her reaction, however, was balanced by the significant number of children who thanked us for talking to them and said they had enjoyed it.

Some questions in the children's interview obtained fuller and more interesting answers than others, but in general we were impressed by the level at which the children were prepared to share their feelings and experience with us. As with all such fieldwork, there is ultimately no way of telling the extent to which respondents are allowing the researcher to enter into their lives, but we are confident that the children attempted to answer the questions as honestly as possible. Evidence for this conclusion comes from the extent to which the children were prepared to share with us intimate details about themselves, their parents and their families. In some cases, the honesty and directness of the children was particularly touching. For instance, in one of the parents' interviews, a mother described how her son had always wanted to go to India to see the Taj Mahal. The boy in question told us that that was what his mother believed, but that he in fact wanted to go to India to see where his natural mother had come from and the kind of life she had lived and the kind of person she would be.

Coding and presentation

The parents' and the children's replies were coded by the interviewer actually during the course of the interviews. Later they were all listened to again by the third member of the team who, not having seen the original coding, re-coded all the interviews. If there was any discrepancy in those two codings, then the relevant answers were listened to by the other member of the team who had an adjudicating decision on how the answer was to be coded. This was only necessary with a relatively small number of answers. There was another small number of answers which were impossible to code either because the parent or the child had not answered the question asked or alternatively because no acceptable decision could be arrived at by the three members of the team.

Some of the questions — particularly those to do with relationships with the child and policies as a parent — were coded individually for mother and father. When parents gave different answers for other questions this was noted.

We have also been very careful not to misrepresent what the parents and the children have told us. In the chapters which follow we have drawn heavily on extracts from interviews with both parents and children. To make this possible, all of the researchers have spent many hours listening and re-listening to tapes in order to get accurate transcripts, and to select good illustrative material. In making our selection we have done our best to extract the typical, rather than the unusual. It would be all too easy to quote the unusual responses, and by doing so to misrepresent the main emphasis of most of the replies.

Finally, in presenting material from the interviews we have sought meticulously not to quote anything which would identify the parties concerned. For this reason some particularly interesting and illuminating material has been omitted from this book. Once or twice we have changed minor factual details in the reported comments to preserve confidentiality. We are sure, however, that in doing this the sense and meaning of the responses have not been altered.

3

The families

Because there are clearly different issues involved, we make a distinction in this stage of the follow-up between those children in the original BAP group who were adopted transracially (e.g., both parents white and the child black or mixed-race) and those children adopted by couples, one or both of whom are black.

Of the original 51 families, 44 were interviewed for this follow-up. Thirty-six of these had adopted transracially and eight were couples in which at least one partner was black. Of the seven families we failed to interview, we were unable to trace four, one was living abroad and one was unwilling to be involved. The response rate is, however, remarkably high considering that it is nearly fifteen years since the parents became involved in the project.

Details of the background and family circumstances of the eight children adopted by black or mixed couples are given in Chapter 11, which concentrates on their experiences. In this and other chapters we concentrate on the 36 families who have adopted transracially and which form the basis of this research.

Marriage breakdown

All of the original adoptive parents of the 36 children are still alive. Thirty-two of the adoptive couples are still together. Four of the 36 families had, by 1974–5, experienced a marriage breakdown. Two of the mothers of this group have remarried and divorced again in the intervening five years; one had remarried before the 1974–5 follow-up and remains married, while the fourth has not remarried, but has established a long-term cohabiting relationship. Four of the study children now live, therefore, in one-parent families, although in at least two of them there is considerable contact with the other parent.[1]

In the four families who experienced divorce before the last follow-up, the study child has lived with the mother. In the two cases of marital breakdown since the last follow-up the study children live with their fathers. In one instance this is apparently because the father lives in a safer, less violent, area; in the other case there are two younger children in the family who have

19

stayed with the mother, whilst the two eldest (including the study child) have gone to live with the father.

Family size

Of the 36 transracial adopters, six were childless at the time of their application to adopt. Only one of these six couples does not now have other children; two had a child of the marriage after adopting, and three adopted a second child. In all these cases the second adopted child was younger than the study child.

Table 3.1 indicates current family size. For those two families which had been split because of marriage breakup it includes all the children of the families because they were in regular contact. Because there was often considerable contact older children living away from home are also included.

Table 3.1   Number of children in the study families

Number of families	Number of children
1	1
9	2
11	3
8	4
5	5
2	6
Total 36	121

Nineteen of the study children are the youngest in the family, 11 are in the middle of the family order and five are the eldest. The remaining child is the one 'only' child.

Occupation and social class of the head of household

At the time of the interviews all the fathers were in employment, but one had received notice of redundancy. The list of occupations includes university lecturer, company director, chartered surveyor, vicar, scientist, engineer, graphic artist, sales manager, computer operator, quality control supervisor, gardener/chauffeur, hotel proprietor, deputy head master, church caretaker and remedial teacher.

Table 3.2 shows the social class of the families, based on the Registrar General's classification of occupations. For the families in which the mother is alone it is based on her occupational position.

Table 3.2 Social class of the study families

Social Class	Number of families
I (professional, etc. occupations)	15
II (intermediate occupations)	14
III (skilled occupations non-manual)	1
III (skilled occupations manual)	3
IV (semi-skilled occupations)	3
Total	36

The families are predominantly social classes I and II, and none come from the numerically more significant social class V.

Mother working outside the home

Thirty of the mothers were working outside the home either part- or full-time. Several were teaching in a range of posts from remedial level to college of further education to remand home. Others included a social worker in a child guidance clinic, dinner lady, shop cleaner, clerical assistant, shop owner and manager. Generally, the mothers seemed to have fulfilled the traditional role of homemaker and main caretaker of the children, while their husbands concentrated on their full-time careers. Generally, the mothers worked part-time in lower status occupations than their husbands, or full-time in jobs such as teaching which left them free during holidays.

Type of housing

Of the 36 families, 28 live in homes they either own or are buying. In addition, three families live in tied accommodation (although two of these own another home), four rent from the local authority and one rents privately. The style of accommodation varies considerably, including rambling Victorian houses, cottages, neat semis and local authority flats. The average size of accommodation is 6.8 rooms per household.[2] On the basis that more than 1.5 people per room is defined as 'overcrowded'[3] none of the families is 'overcrowded'. Indeed, for some of the families the amount of accommodation at their disposal was quite considerable.

Serious ill-health in the family

We asked the parents whether there had been any serious ill-health in the family (excluding the study child) in the previous five years. Eight of the 36 families reported some such ill-health, including psychiatric difficulties of an elder sister to the study child, a sister with asthma and a mother in hospital for an emergency gynaecological operation. But the majority of the study families seemed to enjoy good health.

Religion

The families present a varied picture of the role that religion plays in their lives. In eight families religion was described as 'very important as a principle of life' and they were involved in a wide range of activities, including Sunday School, church services and wives' groups. In four families religion was described as being 'fairly important' usually with some organised involvement. In six families religion was 'not very important', but sometimes with some organised involvement. Eleven families felt that religion was of no importance and had no organised involvement. For the remainder there was no single 'family approach', although individual members were sometimes involved in church activities.

The children

Of the 36 children, 22 are girls and 14 are boys. All except one were still with their adoptive parents at the time of the interview. The one exception was in the care of the local authority.

Age at placement
Table 3.3 indicates the ages that the 36 children were at placement with their adoptive parents.

Table 3.3   Age of study children at placement

Age	Number of children
6 wks–2 mths	7
3 mths–5 mths	13
6 mths–8 mths	7
9 mths–11 mths	4
12 mths–24 mths	5
Total	36

Age at interview
By the time the children were interviewed for the present study their ages were as follows:

Table 3.4   Age of study children at time of interviews

Age	Boys	Girls
12 yrs	1	2
13 yrs	2	6
14 yrs	10	8
15 yrs	0	6
16 yrs	1	0
Totals	14	22

Natural parents
Seventeen of the 36 children are mixed-race in the sense that one natural parent was white. For 15 the white parent was the mother; in two cases it was

Table 3.5   Racial background of natural parents

	Fathers	Mothers
Indian	15	11
English/Irish	2	14
Pakistani	3	1
Singalese	2	1
West Indian	3	1
African	3	0
American negro	2	0
West Indian negro	1	1
Ugandan Asian	1	1
Jamaican Jewish	1	0
Arab	1	0
Indian–French	1	0
Indian–Portugese	0	1
African–Portugese	1	0
African Lebanese	0	1
Chinese Malay	0	1
Chinese Jamaican	0	1
Persian	0	1
Anglo–Polish	0	1
Totals	36	36

23

the father. Only 11 of the 36 had natural parents from the same racial and cultural background. Full details, derived from data collected in previous stages of the BAP research are given in Table 3.5.

The most striking feature of the table is the enormous variety of racial backgrounds represented in the study group. Twenty-two of the 36 children are either Asian or Anglo–Asian in background, seven are African, Afro–Caribbean, Anglo–African or Anglo–Afro–Caribbean; four are mixed Afro–Asian, one is Persian–Asian and one is Chinese Malay–Arab.

Physical appearance

Although 17 of the children had one white natural parent, almost all of them appeared at the time of the interview clearly to be of a different racial background from their adoptive parents.

Health

All of the study children were described by their parents as being generally in good health. Only nine had had a significant illness in the previous five years. These included two for whom asthma was a problem and children who had suffered from either glandular fever or bronchitis.

Education

We received completed questionnaires from the schools of 32 of the 36 children (see Chapter 5). The parents of one child were unwilling for us to contact the school and three schools did not return questionnaires. Twenty-seven of the schools are maintained by the local authority, four are independent and one is voluntary-aided.

On the school questionnaire we asked how many black pupils there were in the school and provided a checklist of different racial backgrounds and combinations of racial backgrounds. We were impressed with the care and accuracy with which the form teachers or their equivalents appeared to fill in these details. Of the 32 schools that replied, four did not answer the question about racial composition; information from the remainder is shown in Table 3.6.

We went on to ask about the number of black children in each child's class or teaching group. Fifteen were the only black child in their class; for six there was one other black child and for four there were two others. Only five study children shared a class with five or more other black children.

These results are of interest at two levels. First, they give an indication of the number of black children that the children were seeing in their daily lives. Second, they give a clue to the racial composition of the areas in which

Table 3.6 Racial composition of
schools attended by the
study children

% of black pupils in school	number of schools
0	6
1	11
2	2
3	0
4	2*
5– 9	3†
10–19	2
20–29	0
30–39	1
40–49	1
Total	28

*both private schools †including one private
school

the children were living. The majority of the children were attending local comprehensive schools, which, it can reasonably be assumed, tend to reflect the racial composition of the areas in which they are located. From Table 3.6 and from other information presented later in the study we can deduce that all but a small proportion of the children were being brought up in primarily white areas.

Representativeness of the BAP group

In this chapter we have introduced the BAP group. Because there are no national data collected on the number of parents who adopt transracially and no information on the characteristics of the parents and children involved in such adoptions, we are not in a position to say exactly how representative our group is.

However, any other study that attempts to examine such adoptions is likely to face problems of bias in the families contacted. Such families, in practice, can only be contacted on an ad hoc basis, through social workers, personal contact or advertising, and there might well be a high refusal rate. This has not been a problem with our study and we have the added advantage of the original information on the natural parents, the children and the adoptive parents at the time of placement.

Also, because our research covers a fairly wide cross-section of families (given that middle-class families have in the past adopted disproportionately to working-class families), family structures, geographical locations and racial backgrounds, we are confident that our research gives as accurate a picture as possible at the present time of the experience of transracial adoption in Britain. It should, however, be remembered that because the number of white babies available for adoption has declined so dramatically in the last 15 years, the characteristics of transracial adoptions may also have changed. For instance, in our sample the majority of parents could produce their own children. In the 1970s, couples who could not produce their own children may have turned to transracial adoption as their only possible means of starting a family.

4

Relationships within the family

In this chapter we begin to explore the experiences of the BAP families and children. Specifically we address ourselves to two of the main criticisms of transracial adoption, those that are related to the child not being seen, and not seeing herself, as 'part of this family'.

The majority of the evidence presented below is based on the words of the parents and children. Most of the parents were relatively articulate when describing their relationship with their children, but the responses of the children, although sometimes detailed, presented two difficulties. First, family life was part of their unquestioned reality. Kitwood, in talking about his research with adolescents, refers to family life as a 'pervasive and some-times relatively featureless part of the taken-for-granted world.'[1] Second, although the children were able to talk about incidents and events, they were sometimes unable to assess the more intangible areas of 'relationships'. This was most apparent with one of the questions early in the children's interview. We asked the children to finish a list of statements including 'my mother thinks I am . . .', 'my father thinks I am . . .', 'my brothers think I am . . .' and 'my form teacher thinks I am . . .'. These questions often failed to get full or related answers; some of the children said they simply did not know. We gained the impression that the further removed from the family the person was, the fuller seemed to be the response. Most of the children found it easier to talk about the views of their form teacher or friends, than about their parents. The results of this question are therefore not used in the analysis that follows.

However, having said this, we believe that the form of questioning developed for the children's interview did allow us to enter into their experience of family life and relationships.

The parents describe their children

Parents were asked: 'How would you describe . . . (child's name) now he/she is growing up? Can you give me an idea of his/her personality?' This was followed by the subsidiary question, 'Can you give a recent event or incident that sums up what you have been saying?' Responses were full and we coded

27

them in the following way: (i) 'positive or generally positive description although some negative characteristics might be described', (ii) response contains 'serious negative characteristics that indicate the parents question the success of the adoption'. Thirty-four of the responses came into the first category. Of the remaining two cases, one was coded as 'both parents give negative descriptions of their child' and in the other the mother's reaction was negative and the father's was positive.

By far the majority of the parents therefore gave either positive or generally positive descriptions of their children.

Mother: What, in one word or . . .

Father: He's so loving, and caring.

Mother: He's a very optimistic child and he sees things from the bright side — very enthusiastic kind of person . . . He's fun-loving and he's got a terrific sense of humour. He's an extremely nice personality.

Interviewer: Can you think of any recent event or thing that he's said that summarises the sort of thing that you'd use to explain to people what he's like?

Mother: What he's like? Um . . . No.

Father: I'm blank now (laughter)

Interviewer: Sometimes something comes to mind.

Mother: Think of little things that, er . . . he's very attentive, too. I can think of something very stupid. I came home last week with very cold feet and he got down and started rubbing and warming my feet. I didn't have to ask, but he just sort of, he looks after us often.

Father: Yes, that's it. Yes, yes. And it's so . . . natural in a way, it's almost . . .

Mother: Yet he's not a goody! I mean . . . he teases us a lot as well.

The large majority of responses were very positive. Some contained negative statements, but the overall perspective seemed to be positive. For example:

Father: She talks to me now, which is something, isn't it? Didn't talk to me, didn't want anything to do with me for years, years. Used to make me angry. Um. Sort of personality?

Mother: She's quite moody.

Father: Yes, she's a bit moody.

Mother: But, then, I think girls, a lot of girls of her age are, you know . . . Um, very similar to . . . (her), you know.

Father: I think she's different with her friends. I think she's quite good fun, actually, with her friends. And she is sometimes, isn't she, at home.

Mother: Oh, she can be, you know, she can be delightful. I mean, she's got into the habit now of — nine times out of ten I'm in bed first before any of them are, you know, and she'll come and sit on the bed with me and she'll talk over what's been going on. You know, she's sort of had sort of a couple of casual boyfriends and she'll come and sit and chat away to me, you know. We sit and have a giggle together. Um, I think it's all part of growing up really, but she, she can be charming and she's . . .

Father: She's much closer to . . . (mother) than she is to me, isn't she?

Mother: Yes.

Some parents talked generally positively about the child, but described her as going through a 'phase'.

Father: She can be 'agin the government' at times, but I don't think any more than the average young person of that age.

Mother: In fact, I think she's beginning to come through that really.

Father: Yes. I think that's so. Yes, it seems to go in fits and starts, but . . . it has declined if you like and she seems generally more helpful around the house, for instance. But I think I would say it was just a phase she was going through. Nothing untoward really.

The above extracts indicate the variety of responses that this question produced, but we are confident that the large majority of parents genuinely felt positive about the children. In the one case where both parents were coded as giving negative descriptions we were also left in no doubt; the mother's responses began with, 'Horrible! Very boring child. Oh yes.'

The next question we asked the parents was, 'How would each of you describe your relationship with . . . (study child)?' This was followed by two supplementary questions, 'Can you give me a recent event or incident that

Table 4.1 Relationship between adoptive parents and children: parents' views

	Fathers	*Mothers*
'Positive' or 'generally positive description but some negative characteristics of relationship described'	32	33
Response indicates serious difficulties in relationship which indicate parents question/ success of adoption	1	3
Impossible to code	1	0
Totals	34*	36

Two of the divorced or separated adoptive fathers were not interviewed

29

describes this?' and 'How does it compare with your relationship with your other children?' In the interviews we made a point of getting *both* parents to describe their relationship and we coded the answers in a similar way to the previous question. Coded responses are shown in Table 4.1.

The majority of parents had positive or generally positive feelings about their relationship with their adopted children:

Father: Well, I suppose mine is the same as it is with the other two children . . .

Interviewer: Would you describe yourself as close to him?

Father: Yes, yes. In as much as, and I don't think he understands this, that I am the solid backbone behind the whole lot. If anything goes wrong, he can turn to me and I'll sort it out. And at the moment he's going through a phase of trying to sort most of the things out himself. Even at school. He only has to come home and tell me what's going on and I really will sort it out. But he hasn't done that yet . . .

Interviewer: How would you describe your relationship with . . . (study child)?

Mother: We get on very well together. I am very, very fond of him and we are very close. He likes to come to a lot of things with me. He always comes to meetings with me. He likes to (feel) wanted and important. He's looking after me.

Father: It doesn't work the same with me because . . .

Mother: He likes to come shopping with me and carry the bags for me. And usually if there's anything worrying him, I can usually get it out of him.

Interviewer: How does your relationship with . . . (study child) compare with your relationship with the other children?

Mother: I think it's about the same really. Except that . . . (study child) physically comes with me more than they do.

Interviewer: Is it possible to compare him with your oldest son?

Mother: . . . (older son) at that age was shyer . . . If I passed . . . (older son) in the street, he didn't like me to wave and say 'Yoohoo', but . . . (study child) will charge across the street!

Father: They are two entirely different characters.

Into the first category we also put responses in which parents described a few negative characteristics, but were 'generally positive' in their responses:

Interviewer: How would you each describe your relationship with him? How do you each get on with him?

Mother: Sometimes I think *I'm* too soft and . . . (husband) too hard, which normally works out as a good medium in the end because he counteracts my softness. It's very very difficult to say, isn't it?

Father: Well, sometimes it's a bit abrasive because I like things like that, you know, and he's a bit . . .

Mother: . . . more lackadaisical.

Father: And that tends to go a little like that, you know.

Interviewer: . . . clash of temperament?

Mother/Father: Yes, yes.

Father: We are somewhat different temperaments. He's a bit laissez-faire and I like it to go like that.

Interviewer: How does it compare with how you got on with . . . (daughter)?

Father: It makes it . . . not to get it out of proportion . . . because some times . . . (study child) and I clash like that, sometimes. I cannot appear to favour . . . (daughter), you see. I have to be, in times like that, equally (strong) with . . . (daughter).

Interviewer: Do you find you are closer to one than the other?

Mother: No, *I* don't. No, not really, because they are so totally different. Their personalities are so totally different. I'm not closer to either of them more than the other.

Finally, here is part of the conversation with one of the mothers whom we coded as having 'serious difficulties in the relationship':

Mother: Difficult. I don't think it's anything to do with him being in his teens. He gets under my skin. To an extent which he shouldn't. Put it another way — an extent to which I shouldn't allow him to do. Because, really, he's no bother. He's not a difficult child. He's not wilfully naughty or disobedient or anything like that. I think probably most of it is my fault. I *oughtn't* to allow him to irritate me to the extent that he does. The rational side of me knows that what's required is a lot more patience and tolerance. I find it very difficult to know why he has this effect on me — whether it's because he's a boy or younger — whether it's a fundamental personality conflict or whether it's simply that there isn't some kind of physical maternal thing.

Obviously, there was a great variety in the content of answers, but, summarising the responses from the parents to these first two questions on the child and their relationships, we can conclude that the large majority of parents talked in positive terms. Where there were negative characteristics described, these were often referred to in terms of the child going through a 'stage'.

We went on to ask parents, 'How like each of you is . . . (child's name) as a person? In what ways is he/she like you?' Again, we asked the question so as to get individual responses from each parent. If there was any doubt about how to code the initial responses of the parents to this question, then we asked them how they would code themselves. Responses are shown in Table 4.2 overleaf.

Table 4.2 Similarities between parents and children: parents' views

	Father	Mother
Very similar or similar in most respects	4	6
Similar in some respects	12	9
Very dissimilar or dissimilar in most respects	13	16
Impossible to code	5	3
Parents could not answer	0	2
Totals	34	36

As can be seen, only a minority of the parents defined their child as being 'similar' or 'very similar' to themselves; 38 per cent of fathers and 44 per cent of mothers felt they were very dissimilar to their children, or dissimilar in most respects.

These responses raise interesting questions. Raynor in her study of 160 sets of parents who had adopted children who had now reached adulthood, found that

> the clearest link between parental satisfaction and any one factor which was explored was the adoptive parents' perception of the child as being similar to them in some way, such as appearance, general intelligence, temperament, mannerism, talents or skills.[2]

In our data, however, although the large majority of the parents described their experience with the adopted child in positive terms, only a minority saw the children as being generally 'like' them as persons. One possible reason for this discrepancy in our data and that collected by Raynor is that she was interviewing the parents of adopted children who had now reached adulthood. There might well be a naturally increased consistency of interpretations of self and children when those children have grown up. The life style, aspirations and relationships of adolescence may produce a perception of being 'different as people'.

This point was nicely illustrated by one of the fathers who compared his older child (now nineteen) with the study child:

> I think it's easier with . . . (older child) because she's now nineteen, she's passed through adolescence into more or less adulthood. I can see (her) growing up into an adult not all that different from us . . . whereas . . . (study child) is still very much in the process of changing from one thing to another. It's hard to say how she'll

end up. She's like a lot of other children; takes a lot of her attitudes and things from us, I think. But that would be surprising if it were different.

Another possible explanation for the discrepancy between our findings and those of Raynor is that families that adopt transracially might well put a positive value on the benefits of diversity within the family and on each individual making a unique contribution. However, whatever the explanation for the feeling of a lack of similarity between the adopted child and its parents, nothing in the present study suggests that this is related to regrets about the adoption and to the lack of strong parent–child relationships.

The children talk about their parents

The children were asked corresponding questions: 'Can you give me an idea of what your Mum is really like as a person?, 'Can you tell me something she has done recently which is a good example of what she is really like? How like your mother are you as a person? Why do you say that?' All were designed to facilitate the children talking and to increase the flow of the interview.

When coding the answers we distinguished between two broad responses: those in which the child was giving a 'positive or generally positive description of the parent and the relationship' and those which indicated a 'poor relationship with the parent'.

Even with a categorisation as basic as this there were still some coding difficulties because several children were only able to produce purely factual descriptions of how the parent spent his/her time and did not appear able to stand back and assess the person and the relationship.

Table 4.3 Relationship between children and adoptive
parents: children's views

	Father	Mother
'Positive' or 'generally positive descriptions of parent and child's relationship with parent'	18	29
Obvious negative descriptions of parent and child's relationship with parent	2	2
Impossible to code	15	5
Totals	35*	36

*This question was omitted for one girl whose parents had divorced

33

The large majority of the children gave responses to both of their parents which were coded as positive or generally positive, although a very much higher proportion of the children gave replies about their fathers which were impossible to classify.

Most children were positive about their mothers:

Girl: She's very considerate. May be not . . . well, she goes to church and she's quite involved in that, and so do my Dad and so do most of the family. I should say more than I am, but I still sort of . . . well, anyway. Yes, she goes to church. Considerate. She's helpful to most people and — well, she doesn't often think of herself, you know; puts others first and, well — do you want to know how she is to me?

Interviewer: Yes. What sorts of things does she do and say and . . .

Girl: Well, she's concerned about me, as any Mum would be. I mean, I don't think 'cos me being adopted has altered anything. I mean, whatever a Mum does, I suppose she does. She, she makes me independent . . . She makes me sort of — she's not as if 'I'll do this for you, I'll do that for you' and, um, she's, she doesn't push me to do things.

Interviewer: How much do you think you are like her as a person?

Girl: Hardly at all, really. Um, I can't, I think, I can't really say what I'm like in comparison with her because I don't know what . . . Am I like her? I don't know. I think I might have the same sense of humour sometimes. I've got quite a good sense of humour and I laugh at most things, um, I don't really know.

And about their fathers:

Girl: I think you got to get — uh, he doesn't often, he never sings, put it that way. He doesn't like making a fool of himself or doesn't like being showy. Um. Kind. Very generous.

Interviewer: Tell me a bit about — why do you say very generous? You said that with a lot of conviction.

Girl: Mm. Well, let's say, um, I was saving up for a new pair of shoes and I had £5 I didn't have and the sale was at the end of the week. He'd either give me a job, which wasn't really worth it, you know, it's only about 50p. -worth and he'd give me £5, or he'd just give it to me and say, you can pay me back later, and he never accepts it afterwards.

Interviewer: This example of a job — has he done that? I mean about the shoes and the job.

Girl: No, he hasn't done it about the shoes, but I was £1 short and he gave me that. A 10p. job just to polish up all the furniture.

Interviewer: That was for shoes, was it?

Girl: No, that was — I can't remember. I think that was for a pair of trousers, which I didn't really need.

Only two gave negative descriptions. For example:

Boy: Um, if I've done something wrong, I mean, if I did something wrong and my brother did the same thing wrong, then I would get a worse punishment than he did.

Interviewer: I see. Let's ask another question. How like you is your Mum?

Boy: Very different.

Interviewer: Is she? In what ways?

*Boy :*Different personality.

Interviewer: How?

Boy: She goes about things in different ways. Say, I mean, I make friends really quite easily considering that I'm brown, I suppose. She'll go about it a different way. She gets friends through other people — I suppose she talks easily to people, I mean . . . She's, I don't know how to say it — different.

But most children gave positive accounts of their relationships with both of their parents. A significant proportion made some critical comments, but typically these were not overriding ones. Many more children had difficulty in assessing their relationship with their father than with their mother.

Relationships with brothers and sisters

We asked the parents, 'How does . . . (study child) get on with his/her brothers and sisters?' One of the children was an only child and the parents of only one of the remaining 35 talked in a way which indicated major problems between siblings. All of the rest described a positive relationship between the children in the family. For example:

Interviewer: How does she get on with the others?

Mother: She does get on well with them really. And more so now because they're more understanding of her — they're older. The oldest one's been home this year and really glad to have been home because, possibly, she didn't get on so well when she was younger. She was the oldest and more bossy. But they've really got to know each other better this year — that's good. . . . (second daughter) was always more motherly towards her. She gets on quite well with . . . (first son) — he's very quiet and patient.

Father: Very often . . . (first son) is the one to play a game with her. No, . . . (second son) does it now! . . . (first son) used to play with her quite a bit. Now it's . . . (second son) and . . . (study child).

Mother: Well, they share information about school, girl-friends and boy-friends. That's what's brought them together. I think she gets on well with them really.

And:

Father: I think fine. It's slightly unfortunate that she and . . . (other daughter) have to share a bedroom and at times they slightly grate on each other.

35

Interviewer: Apart from slight tensions, things are . . .

Father: Very good.

Mother: They went through a bad patch and they seemed to squabble. She and . . . (other daughter) had terrible 'do's' in the bedroom and . . . (other daughter) would come out crying, saying, 'I just hated her, Mummy. I wanted to hit her.' But that's blown over now.

Father: She always got on very well with . . . (son).

Mother: The boys . . . they're very fond of . . . (study child).

Interviewer: Does . . . (other daughter) say anything?

Mother: No, she never does.

Reviewing the parents' responses on relations between the study child and her brothers or sisters, it is clear that the large majority regard these relationships as favourable and positive. There were references to disagreements and 'squabbles', but these were usually referred to as just being 'a stage' the children were going through, and part of the normal relationships between siblings. Some of the parents described the study child as being closer to one brother or sister than to others, but such characteristics would be normal for biologically-related brothers and sisters. Indeed, some of the parents volunteered the remark that the relationships were 'just like any brother or sister'.

The children were also asked to describe their reactions to their brothers and sisters. Some had difficulty in expressing their feelings, and gave simple factual descriptions instead. The majority, however, described very positive relationships with siblings:

Girl: She's good fun . . . Uh, she treats me as near her age, I mean there's about four years' gap, but she treats me more as if I were older.

Interviewer: Right. And d'you do a lot of things together?

Girl: Yes.

Interviewer: What kind of things do you like doing together?

Girl: Uh, I like going shopping with her and — I mean, if we go shopping for clothes, I prefer to go with her, sort of thing, like that.

Only seven children (two boys and five girls) talked in 'obviously negative' terms about a brother or sister. Of these, however, three had other brothers or sisters with whom they had a much better relationship. Generally speaking, the adopted children appeared to get on very well with other children in the family.

Experience of family life

Two devices were used to assess the children's experience of family life: *specific questions and situations* and *family integration statements*. The first of these was to present the children with four situations aimed at assessing the child's experience of somebody *knowing* them, somebody *being happy* for them, somebody whom they could *confide* in and somebody who would *sort things out* for them. We regarded these as crucial elements of a child's experience of successful family relations.

1 Somebody 'knows' them

The children were asked: 'Of all the people in the family and outside, who knows best what you're really like as a person?' 32 of the 36 children gave a positive answer, indicating somebody knew what they were 'really like as a person'. Of these, 26 specifically referred to a member of the family. Four responses (three boys and one girl) were uncertain or negative, indicating doubt that anyone knew what they were really like.

2 Somebody is happy for them

The next question we asked was, 'If you were really happy about something that had gone right for you, which person inside or outside the family would you want to be the first to know?' Thirty-three felt that there was someone they would wish to tell and 25 of these were in the family.

3 Somebody to confide in

The third question of this kind that we asked the children was, 'If you were really worried about something personal, who would you go to talk about it to?' Thirty-one children felt there was someone to whom they could turn, of whom 27 were in the immediate family. Mothers were by far the most important 'listeners'; fathers were mentioned only rarely.

The results of this question are generally consistent with the earlier two, although it is interesting that a slightly higher number of the children say there is 'no one' to confide in. And a disproportionate number of these are boys.

4 Someone to 'sort things out'

The final question in this group was, 'If you were wrongly accused of stealing something from a local shop, who would you go to to sort things out?' Thirty-one of the children felt there was someone who would 'stick up for them and sort things out': three did not. Again, the large majority (27) felt able to turn to members of the family for support.

The results for the above four questions give further evidence of the children's perceptions of family members and relationships. Only eight of the children (three girls and five boys) indicated having any difficulty with having someone who knows them, someone who is happy for them, someone to confide in and someone who would sort things out for them. The remainder felt there was someone to turn to in each of these circumstances, and for the vast majority support was to be found within the family itself.

Family Integration Statements

Next, the children were presented with eight statements and asked to tick whether they strongly agreed, disagreed, strongly disagreed or were uncertain. The statements were designed not only to cover the central areas of family life and relationships, but also to incorporate the fact that these were adoptive families. They were also designed so that the children might compare their own family circumstances with those of their peers. For

Table 4.4 Children's responses to Family Integration Statements

Statement	Boys (n = 14)			Girls (n = 22)		
	Agree	Un-Certain	Dis-agree	Agree	Un-certain	Dis-agree
I enjoy family life	10	3	1	20	1	1
I would like to leave home as soon as possible when I'm able to	1	5	8	5	2	15
Most families are happier than ours	2	4	8	0	1	21
People in our family trust one another	8	2	4	16	5	1
I am treated in the same way as my brother and sister	6	2	6	21	0	0*
Most people are closer to their parents than I am	4	4	6	4	0	18
If I am in trouble I know my parents will stick by me	10	4	0	19	3	0
My parents know what I am really like as a person	10	2	2	18	3	1

*n = 21 because one girl was an only child

analysis the categories of 'strongly agree' and 'agree' have been combined, as have the categories 'strongly disagree' and 'disagree'.

The responses to these statements appear to show a general picture of family integration of these children with only a small number of children obtaining relatively low scores. There does, however, appear to be a difference between boys and girls on some of these questions. The four children showing the lowest Family Integration Scores are all boys.

Summary

Within the BAP group there is a wide variety of families and family styles. Differences of class, income, occupation, mothers working, family size, ages of children and ages between children all must play their part in determining patterns of family relationships. Our task, therefore, in this chapter has not been to analyse the intricacies of individual family patterns and processes, but to present an overall view of family relations for the group.

By a combination of methods we have attempted to assess family relations from the perspectives both of parents and children. For the majority of families there seems a consistent and happy picture of the parents and the children defining each other in a mutually warm, supportive, caring and positive way. In addition to this, the more specific questions we asked suggest that the majority of the children see their families as places in which they are understood, cared for, have the possibility of confiding and know that others will support them or 'take their side'. A generally happy picture emerges too when the children are asked to define their family in comparison with that of others and also their position in the family compared with the position of brothers and sisters.

The evidence presented in this chapter does, however, point to a small group of the BAP children for whom the picture is perhaps a less happy one, although the evidence of difficulties is in some cases very limited. By looking at all the responses relating to each specific child we can gain an idea of the number of children who appear to be experiencing difficulties within the family (see Table 4.5). More boys than girls appeared to be having difficulties in some areas of family life, but for at least half of the boys (seven) there is no evidence of any difficulties in family relationships. Only two of the boys came up with problematic responses for more than half of the questions asked. One of these has a history of being taken into and out of the care of the local authority. As far as we are aware this boy is the only child of the BAP for whom substitute care has at any time had to be found.

For none of the girls is there a majority of problematic responses. Two of the girls have two problematic responses and a further three expressed difficulties on individual measures.

Table 4.5 focuses upon the 12 children for whom, on the basis of evidence presented in this chapter, there appear to be difficulties.

Table 4.5 Twelve children showing difficulties in family relationships

	Boys							Girls				
	1	2	3	4	5	6	7	8	9	10	11	12
Parents define child negatively	X							X				
At least one parent defines relationship negatively	X	X						X				
Parents define relationship with siblings negatively	X											
Child defines mother negatively		X	X									
Child defines father negatively	X			X								
Child defines relationship with at least one sibling negatively	X		X						X	X		
No one understands them	X	X			X						X	
No one is happy for them	X	X										
No one to confide in		X	X		X	X			X			
No one to sort things out	X					X						X
Low family integration score (e.g., half score or less)	X	X		X			X					
No. of difficulties for each child	9	6	3	2	2	2	1	2	2	1	1	1

Again, it must be stressed that the majority of these 12 are only giving limited evidence of difficulties in certain areas of family relationships. This finding seems roughly comparable, or indeed favourable by comparison, to what is known about relationships in other adoptive families. For instance, Raynor, in her retrospective study of grown-up adoptees says:

more than two-thirds of the parents, but only half the young people assessed their

40

relationships as close during all the years that the child was growing up in the family.

And she also notes:

> In addition to those parents who had a close relationship with their child, there were others who had felt this way except during the child's adolescence.[3]

Although it is important not to over-estimate the differences, our finding of more of the boys indicating problematic areas of family relationships is consistent with earlier studies of white children adopted by white families.[4]

Of the 12 children experiencing some difficulties in family relationships, four were of mixed-race natural parentage, whereas there were 17 out of 36 in the whole group. There seems no evidence, therefore, of a definite pattern in this respect.

In this chapter we have presented our initial findings relating to the family life of the children. In later chapters we shall examine in more detail some of the specific aspects of family life — particularly those relating to the handling and definition of racial background. However, on the basis of the evidence presented so far we must conclude that there is little evidence of more problematic family relationships for our group of transracially-adopted children than for groups of white children adopted by white families. We can also find little evidence of the family fragmentation and personal isolation which the critics of transracial adoption have claimed.

5

The child outside the family

A second criticism of transracial adoption is that the child will be unable to operate effectively in a white society. Although relationships may be favourable within the family, the child will be unable to develop satisfactory relationships in the outside world.

The children in our study are of course still in many ways protected by their families, but they are beginning to take the first major steps to independence. They have a network of friends and acquaintances; participate in activities such as sport and music in which they are measured on their own merit; organise large amounts of their own time; and now that they are at secondary school they often mix with staff and other youngsters who do not know their parents and sometimes are not aware of their adoptive status. They are increasingly seen as individuals in their own right.

This independence is showing itself not only socially but academically. The young people are selecting subjects and courses of study which will significantly affect their future. They are entering a period of their lives in which academic motivation will be very important.

In this chapter, therefore, we examine the children's peer-group relationships and also their academic progress. We do this by combining data from three sources (the parents' interviews, the children's interviews and the school questionnaire).

Other black children as friends

In order to set the scene we asked each child if she had any 'coloured/brown/black' friends. Table 5.1 on the facing page indicates that more than half of the children said they had no black friends, and the majority of the remainder had only a limited number. This information appears consistent with the details given in Chapter 3 about the number of black children in the schools and classes. It again highlights the fact that these children were living in a primarily white social world.

Peer-group relationships: parents' responses

The parents were asked a group of questions on different aspects of their

Table 5.1   Number of black friends

	Boys	Girls	Total
None	9	13	22
1	2	4	6
2–5	3	2	5
More than 5	–	2	2
Not asked	–	1	1
Totals	14	22	36

child's relationships: Has he/she got any friends at school? Does he/she prefer boys/girls of his/her own age or does he/she prefer those who are older or younger? Does he/she ever see them outside school? How often? What about friends who live nearby? Do his/her friends ever call for him/her? How do you think he/she gets on with other boys and girls? Is he/she a good mixer? Or does he/she prefer to do things on his/her own? Does he/she tend to be a follower or a leader? Can he/she keep friends?

The responses were coded on a simple three-point scale: 'Positive description of peer relations', 'Generally positive description of peer relations, but some difficulties described', 'Serious difficulties in peer relations'.

Table 5.2 summarises the replies:

Table 5.2   Study children's peer-group relationships: parents' view

	Boys	Girls	Total
Positive description	11	19	30
Positive, some difficulties	1	3	4
Serious difficulties	2	0	2
Totals	14	22	36

The large majority of parents described their child's peer relations in positive terms. For example, the mother of one boy commented:

Mother: He has hordes of them.
Interviewer: Does he bring them round?
Mother: Yes. And they're long-term friends. He's had them all through his childhood.
Interviewer: Is he a follower or a leader?
Mother: A leader. I'm always ticking him off for bringing them home. He never walks in the door without bringing somebody. I'm always having to send them home.

43

Interviewer: Do you approve of them or does he pick up all sorts of friends?

Mother: No. I approve of them. They're basically very nice boys and I've seen them since they were in short trousers. Yes. They're all very nice boys. I do approve of them. It's nice to see what they're mixing with.

In some cases replies were 'generally positive but with some difficulties':

Interviewer: Can you tell me about her friends? Does she have a best friend or a gang of school friends?

Mother: I think she is fairly popular.

Father: Yes. There's the friend with whom she goes to . . . Not quite as friendly as the girl down the road — they very often go by car in the mornings. This girl comes round quite frequently. It's more that way round. She's more selfish. She waits for people to come to her rather than going . . .

Interviewer: Is she a follower or a leader?

Father: If anything, more a leader.

Mother: I think in many ways she is.

Interviewer: Do you like her friends or does she choose people you'd rather . . . that you disapprove of?

Father: One or two that we're not quite so happy with because we believe they're not such a good influence, but in general . . .

Mother: I think she's in a class . . . which are not quite as able and they are a naughty class. If she had just made perhaps a higher class, she'd have made different friends. Sometimes I think it would have been better.

Two expressed 'serious difficulties':

Mother: None, I would say. Nobody looks, really looks, bothered about him.

Father: No. No. He did spend this odd day with this . . .

Mother: Yes. But then, you see, he makes such demands on them that they drop him.

Father: If he does make friends, he loses them because of the demands he makes on them, or has made on them.

Children's responses

The children were also asked a cluster of questions about their friendships: Do you go around in a group or just with one or two friends? What do you like doing together? Do you have a best friend? What do you like about him/her? What colour is he/she? How many coloured/black/brown friends do you have? Do you bring your friends home? Do your parents like your friends? Once again, a single coding was given on the basis of all the responses, and these are shown in Table 5.3:

Table 5.3 Study children's peer-group relationships: children's view

	Boys	Girls	Total
Positive description	8	21	29
Generally positive, some difficulties	4	0	4
Serious difficulties	0	0	0
Impossible to code	2	1	3
Totals	14	22	36

Again, the large majority of children were coded as giving positive descriptions of peer-group relations:

Girl: Most of the time I go around with one friend who's doing all the same set subjects as I am. We live near each other and like the same things. At school, we go round in a group.
Interviewer: Tell me about the special friend.
Girl: Charlotte. I see a lot of her.
Interviewer: What do you like doing together?
Girl: We've been ice-skating. We've been to the cinema.
Interviewer: Do your friends come home?
Girl: Yes, they do. Quite a lot.
Interviewer: Does your Mum like them?
Girl: Yes.

And another girl, when asked to tell us something about her friends:

Girl: I'm rather fickle about them. I'm always going off them and then liking them. There's this girl, Tessa, who — I wouldn't really class her as my best friend, but I go around with her a lot because nobody else will go around with her — she's not very popular; she's a bit immature and she annoys people and I feel sorry for her so . . .
She goes around with me quite a lot. I like being in quite a big group because I think it's more fun, although I do like to have a best friend. I think Jenny Brown, this girl, is my best friend at school, but out of school I'd say Anna — my next-door neighbour and Jessica are my best friends.
Interviewer: What sort of things do you like doing together?
Girl: I like going to the cinema, going shopping. We sometimes go to discos and things.
Interviewer: And do you have a particular best friend out of that lot? Or are they best friends for different reasons?
Girl: Yes.
Interviewer: Say, Anna, your next-door neighbour — what sort of things do you like about her?

Girl: She's a nice person to talk to. She's got a nice personality. I like her family as well. It's good because we live so close so we can arrange things at the last minute. I think we're quite alike. Well, she doesn't look like me — she's got blonde hair.

Interviewer: What sort of things do you like about Jessica?

Girl: She's very extrovert. I like her for that. I suppose I admire her quite a lot for that. She can go up and talk to anybody and just start joking and things like that. Whereas I can't, but when I'm with her, I'm more out-going. I like her family as well. She's just nice to be with. Good fun.

A small number appeared to have generally good relationships with friends, but with some difficulties:

Boy: Well, one or two. There's one, Robert Hudson, who goes round with them — he's in my chemistry set — he asks me for the answers. We're good friends by ourselves, but when we're with the other people, he's sort of with *them*.

Interviewer: I see. Do you go round in a group or just one or two people?

Boy: When I go to school — break-times and things like that — I normally find myself into the library so I can work, but apart from that I'm normally with a group. Sometimes there's a group of three, quite intelligent, very day-dreamy and I join in with their conversation because it's just different from school.

Interviewer: Would you say you had a best friend?

Boy: Yes. He's an adopted boy — surprisingly. I've known him since about two. We used to go to the same playgroup . . . I find it more fun in their family than in mine.

Interviewer: Do you have friends home from school?

Boy: Not now. I never get round to inviting them because I'm ashamed of my Mum. And I never get invited to theirs.

Interviewer: Do your parents like your friends?

Boy: Mum doesn't — no, not really. Unless she knows the Mum and Dad of that child.

Peer-relations: teacher responses

A third view of the child's peer-group relationships was obtained by asking teachers to compare the study-child's popularity with that of other pupils of the same age at school. Of the 32 responses, the majority were average or above (Table 5.4).

There was also a space for teachers to make general comments about the child's social progress. Many took the opportunity to support their positive ratings with comments such as the following:

. . . appears to be a happy, well-adjusted child with a wide circle of friends.

In short, he is a very popular boy, whose company is sought by other students.

Table 5.4 Popularity of study children at school: teachers' views

	Boys	Girls	Total
Amongst most popular	0	2	2
Above average	5	7	12
Average	6	8	14
Below average	1	1	2
Amongst least popular	1	1	2
Totals	13	19	32

An excellent pupil who seems well-integrated, self-confident and well-adapted.

. . . is a polite, well-spoken, delightful pupil, quite at home with people of his own age or adults.

Those children (four) who received below-average ratings received comments like the following:

Since she has joined the school, she has tended to remain solitary. Her friends are at the Church club at which she is an active member.

It has been noticeable that she can relate very well to others on only very few occasions. Very many different approaches have been tried with only limited success.

Comparison of peer-group relationship ratings

As in the previous chapter, we have combined the data about peer-group relationships to give an overall view.

Again, boys seem to experience more difficulties. One boy was described by his parents and described himself as having difficulties; one was referred to by parents as having difficulties, three others saw themselves as having some difficulties, and a further two were described by teachers as below average in popularity. But again these combined results should be treated with caution. Although seven of the boys have a problematic response in one of these categories, only one child defines himself as having difficulties which are confirmed by both parents and teacher. And indeed in any sample of children of the same age as the BAP group it would obviously be expected that some children would be rated as below average in popularity. Only two girls receive problematic responses: both of these were described as below average in popularity. Of these nine children for whom there is an indication of some difficulties, four are of mixed-race parentage.

Comparing the overall peer-group responses with those concerning family relationships there seems to be some consistency. Not only do boys appear disproportionately in both sets of problematic responses, but the boy who had the highest number of problematic family relationships responses also had two out of three problematic peer-group relationship responses; the boy with the next highest number of problematic family relationship responses referred himself to some difficulties in peer-group relations.

However, even given that a disproportionate number of boys seem to experience limited difficulties in peer-group relationships, we again conclude that the picture is a generally positive and happy one and that we can find no general evidence of difficulties in peer-group relationships.

'Girlfriends' and 'boyfriends'

Another aspect of peer relationships which we attempted to explore was whether the study group had 'girlfriends' or 'boyfriends'. We first asked if their group of friends had girlfriends or boyfriends. If the answer was 'no', the subject was not pursued unless the child herself commented further. If the answer was 'yes', the child was asked, 'Do *you* have a boyfriend/girlfriend?' and if the answer to this question was 'yes' we asked for a description of him/her. By building on the questions in this way we hoped to let the child set the pace.

For many children it was clearly too early: others were content to observe from the fringes, watching friends form liaisons. A few said they did have boyfriends or girlfriends.

Table 5.5   Boyfriends and girlfriends of the study children

	Boys	Girls	Total
Friends have boyfriend or girlfriend	6	11	17
Some do; some don't	1	5	6
None do	7	6	13
BAP child has boyfriend or girlfriend	3	4	7

The way the children answered, as illustrated in the following extracts, confirmed our expectations that for most children, members of the opposite sex were seen as friends or as the object of a 'crush' rather than as a 'boyfriend' or 'girlfriend'.

Interviewer: Do any of your friends have girlfriends?
Boy: They've got girl friends, not as 'girlfriends', but friends who are girls.

And:

> *Boy:* No. I can't see why you need a girlfriend at the age of fourteen.
> *Interviewer:* Do your friends have girlfriends?
> *Boy:* I don't think most of them do.
> *Interviewer:* Have you got a girlfriend? Do you want to?
> *Boy:* I wouldn't mind.
> *Interviewer:* Have you gone out of your way to find one?
> *Boy:* No. I'll wait and see what comes along.

For a few of the children the subject of boyfriends/girlfriends was of more concern, or at least they were more articulate about it:

> *Girl:* No. Not at the moment.
> *Interviewer:* Did you have last week?
> *Girl:* Well, yes. Not last week. He was black; I found him. He's in the year below me, though, and we didn't get on that well.
> *Interviewer:* Do you think it makes any difference being (black) and getting boyfriends?
> *Girl:* Yes. I think it does make a difference. Most of the boys in my year are just friends: I wouldn't want to go out with them and they wouldn't want to go out with me. I think that it might make a bit of difference, but if they really liked me, I don't think it would have done.

In only one case did a child describe difficulties in relationships which were more directly related to racial background:

> *Boy:* I found out the hard way. I tried to get a girlfriend. I tried three girls and they all said 'no'. The last one I tried I had become really attached to her and she was a very good friend of mine. We always used to go around with each other and I knew she liked me and I phoned her up one day and I said, 'Would you go out with me?' and she said, 'Yes'. And then, the next day, she was moaning about and I went up to her and said, 'What's wrong?' and she said, 'I'm not going out with you.' I said, 'Why not?' and she just walked away. And eventually at the end of school I went up to her and asked her, 'Why won't you go out with me?' and she wouldn't tell me and eventually I forced her and she said, 'Because you're coloured'. And that really did hurt. For the first time it really hurt.
> *Interviewer:* Did she explain? Was that her feelings or her parents?
> *Boy:* She didn't say. She said it was *her* feelings, but I don't think it was. And that's what really hurt. I don't think it was her who was saying it. Because of that we've completely lost touch and I wanted to stay friends with her after she left school.

This experience was obviously distressing and it is all the more poignant because it encapsulates what some commentators fear will happen to all transracially adopted young people in the sphere of heterosexual relationships. On the other hand, there is no evidence that this experience

49

was the direct product of being transracially adopted. It could well be simply the result of being black in a white society. However, the chances of these children meeting 'boyfriends' and 'girlfriends' of the same racial background were, of course, very limited compared with their contemporaries growing up in the black community. What is clear from the responses to this question is that for the majority of the children having 'boyfriends' and 'girlfriends', and the problems this may produce, are a thing of the future.

Aspects of racial background in school

Although the subjects of racial difference and the impact of colour on the lives of the BAP families will be dealt with in detail in later chapters, it is appropriate to examine here the particular aspects of racial background which relate to the school.

Teachers were asked, 'Does his/her colour give him/her any difficulties at school?' They were asked to tick one of three responses and the results were as follows:

Table 5.6   Teachers' assessment of difficulties faced by children at school

	Boys	Girls	Total
No difficulties	10	17	27
Some, but not many, difficulties	3	2	5
Many difficulties	0	0	0
Totals	13	19	32

The majority of children (27) were thought to experience no difficulties at school relating to colour; only five were described as having some, but not many, difficulties. Interestingly, only one of these children (a girl) was described by a teacher as being amongst the least popular. The remaining four who were thought to be having some difficulties were described as average in popularity (two boys) and above average in popularity (one boy, one girl). The difficulties appear to be linked to specific incidents rather than to a general isolation in the school.

The teachers were asked to comment on their responses. The following are representative of the comments which saw no difficulties:

Because of her colour she is easily identified among a crowd of white children and thus her misbehaviour is easily detected. This apart, there seems to be no problem attributable to her colour in her relationships with teachers and the peer group, by whom she seems to be accepted.

And:

> With so few non-white pupils in the school, which is in a rural commuter belt of largely middle-class families, integration is no problem within the school.

Others who thought there were some difficulties commented in the following ways:

> (He) is teased by certain members of the form and some outsiders because of the colour of his skin. However, other members of the form are teased to a similar degree because of religion, spots, wearing glasses, smallness, etc. (He) does not appear to find the situation stressful as he is capable of defending himself both verbally and physically.

And:

> He is a well-liked and accepted member of his form, but it would be naive to suggest that he does not encounter any such problems outside the classroom.

The parents' view

We asked parents, 'How has his/her colour been dealt with by the staff at the secondary school he/she is attending? Well or badly?'

The interviewer instructions were to establish whether the parents were satisfied, and if not, why. We were interested to know, for instance, if any parents would feel the school had not done enough to promote cultural and racial pride. We also wanted to know how the parents felt about the school's handling of any specific incidents of aggression or hostility.

Table 5.7 School handling of colour: parents' views

	Boys	Girls	Total
Handled well	8	10	18
Handled 'in between'	1	1	2
Handled badly	1	0	1
Not an issue	3	9	12
Impossible to code	1	2	3
Totals	14	22	36

The parents, on the whole, were satisfied with the schools' handling of situations that did arise and were content with the status quo if race and colour had 'not been an issue'. The parents' responses reflect the general feeling that a passive attitude to racial background within the school was

51

acceptable. There was no general feeling that the schools could or should do more to promote racial pride or awareness.

The children's view

A further potential difficulty related to colour was explored with the children when they were asked, 'Do you think that teachers treat you any differently at school because of your colour?' A large majority (32) answered 'no'; only four answered 'yes'. Of the four, three felt that the difference in treatment was somewhat preferential:

Interviewer: Can you tell me about the teachers in school. Have they ever treated you differently because you're coloured?

Boy: I think they have, but the thing is, that I think they've treated me *better* because I'm coloured.

Interviewer: So they are extra careful not to look as though they might be being nasty to you?

Boy: No. I think they realise I could have troubles in school and because of it they look after me better.

Interviewer: What? They make sure the other kids aren't nasty?

Boy: It's like my form teacher — well, all through — when I'm a bit down, they can tell and they always say, 'Right . . . (boy's name). Don't go to assembly, come here, is there anything worrying you?' They always ask me.

The remaining child's response describes treatment which implies suspicion and lower expectations for black children:

Interviewer: Do you think teachers treat you differently because of it (racial background)?

Boy: Not now. I mean, I can tell they trust me now. If there's anybody to go and open the cupboards — usually I am the person to get it, or some girl.

Interviewer: When you say 'now', do you mean that in the past . . . ?

Boy: No. At the beginning of school when they didn't know you, they would separate you, the coloureds, from the whites and say, 'You've got to watch them carefully until they're proved themselves, until they're as good as the whites'.

Interviewer: Who were they saying that to? Amongst themselves?

Boy: No. I think that's what they would say. They put you in the lower sets and watch you all the time.

This last response was very much an isolated one. The large majority of children reported no problems with school staff related to their racial background.

Academic progress: parent responses

From the parents' point of view there are two important aspects to the academic side of school life: how they see the child's ability in comparison with others of his age-group and, taking into account his ability, how satisfied they are with the child's progress.

Table 5.8   Parents' assessment of children's ability

	Boys	Girls	Total
Amongst the most able	3	6	9
Above average	2	6	8
Average	4	7	11
Below average	3	2	5
Amongst least able	1	1	2
Impossible to code	1	0	1
Totals	14	22	36

As a group, the children were rated fairly highly by their parents, with nearly half described as above average or amongst the most able. The boys show a fairly even distribution, with four described as average, five above, and four below. The girls, on the other hand, have more than half of their number in the 'above average'/'amongst most able' categories. Only three out of 22 girls are described as 'below average' or 'amongst the least able'.

Teacher responses

A useful direct comparison can be made by looking at the teacher responses to the question, 'How would you rate his/her academic ability compared with other pupils of the same age at your school?' This question produced the following results:

Table 5.9   Teachers' assessments of children's ability

	Boys	Girls	Total
Amongst most able	1	8	9
Above average	3	2	5
Average	5	8	13
Below average	3	1	4
Amongst least able	1	0	1
Totals	13	19	32

By comparison with parental ratings, the group (as might be expected) received slightly lower ratings from teachers than from parents, but the numbers considered amongst most able (nine) and above average (five) are impressive. The boys represent a perfect normal distribution around the average with four above average, five average and four below average. The girls receive proportionately higher ratings with ten above average, eight average and only one below average. The number of girls described by teachers as amongst the most able (eight) seems really rather remarkable.

Satisfaction with progress: parent responses

The other aspect of the parents' view of progress is how satisfied or happy they are with the progress, taking into account their perception of the child's ability. Table 5.10 indicates the parents' responses:

Table 5.10 Parents' satisfaction with educational progress

	Boys	Girls	Total
Happy with progress	5	14	19
Mainly happy with progress	5	5	10
Unhappy with progress	3	3	6
Impossible to code	1	0	1
Totals	14	22	36

The majority of parents (29) were happy or mainly happy with their child's progress. Of the six children whose parents were unhappy about their progress at school, there was an equal number of boys and girls. One of the six (a girl) was described by her parents as being above average in ability, but the remaining five were all described by parents as 'below average' or 'amongst the least able'.

Teachers' assessment of children's effort

Another measure of the child's adjustment at school is the amount of 'effort' the child puts into his school work. Teachers were asked to assess the child's 'effort' in comparison with his peers on a scale ranging from the most to the least hard-working (Table 5.11).

The majority of the children were described as above average in the effort they put into school work, with a small number (five) described as below average. This result seems to indicate that the children not only have the ability to perform effectively at school, but also have the motivation to

Table 5.11 Children's effort at school: teachers' assessments

	Boys	Girls	Total
Most hard-working	3	9	12
Above average	4	6	10
Average	3	2	5
Below average	3	2	5
Amongst least hard-working	0	0	0
Totals	13	19	32

channel their energy and talent into school work. Once again, there are proportionately more girls at the high end of the table.

Summary

In this chapter we have taken our description of the BAP families a stage further and asked how the children are faring outside the home. By combining the responses of parents, teachers and the children we have developed a picture of this area of the children's lives.

The children are all living in a predominantly white world. The racial composition of the schools is mirrored by the children's responses relating to the racial background of their friends. A majority had no black friends at all and all but two had a very limited number.

Yet the overall finding from the questions about peer-group relations is that the children are integrated into the social world in which they find themselves. There are, of course, exceptions and peer-group relations are not, of course, always straightforward. But for the large majority of children there is no evidence to support those who have anticipated that peer-group relationships would be problematic for the transracially-adopted adolescent.

Nor is there any evidence to suggest that life is so difficult for such children that they will be unable to operate effectively at school. If anything, the evidence on academic progress at least seems to be that these children are on average doing rather well.

As a group, the children's abilities are rated relatively highly by both parents and teachers; most of the children are described as average or above average in ability. Parents on the whole are happy with their child's progress. A large majority of children are described as average or above average in the effort they put into their school work. They compare favourably with peers in ability and seem able to channel their energies into school work.

As in our findings about relationships within the family, the picture seems somewhat less happy for boys than for girls. But again, this has to be kept in perspective. The majority of responses relating to boys as well as girls outside the home indicate that they are not experiencing difficulties.

6

The family approach to racial background

So far we have described the 36 families and children in general terms. Most of the data we have presented could equally well have been collected on any group of adolescents growing up in their families. But there is something special about the children in our group. All of them have a completely or partly different racial background to their adoptive parents. It is to this that we must now turn.

One of the central social work approaches to transracial placement has seen it as necessary for the child to develop a sense of 'identity' with her racial background. It is felt that such a sense of identity, and a pride in her racial heritage, are crucial to the psychological well-being of the child and her ability to function effectively in a world where many people will categorise her on the basis of her colour. For instance, the adoption support group PPIAS write in a statement about the adoption of black children by white parents:

> The great majority of mixed-race families have learned that it is simply not enough to demonstrate pride and affection for our children within the family circle. We have to use our initiative and imagination to reinforce our children's pride in themselves and the pleasure they take in their ethnic minority roots.[1]

Indeed, those people who have regarded transracial adoption as dangerous and problematic have regarded the issue of 'identity' as central. For instance, Chestang, in his critique of transracial adoption in the United States ten years ago, wrote:

> (that) a child reared in a white family will lose contact with the black experience and will be unprepared to deal with the exigencies of black life is a concern that cannot be treated lightly. Having been socialized largely to the white experience, such a child is likely to experience an identity crisis throughout his life; thus he will be truly fragmented.[2]

Nearer to home and more recently, Samuels has argued

> The black person is still painfully vulnerable to rejection which white people find difficult to understand . . . He is bound to undergo severe psychological and emotional problems of identity. Racially black and culturally white, what is his cultural inheritance?[3]

In this chapter we shall look, therefore, at how the parents in our group have handled their children's different racial background and what their policies have been on the issue of racial identity.

Families, following the theoretical approach of Berger and Luckman, can be regarded as 'negotiators of reality.[4] White parents who adopt black children are in a position, at least in the early years of childhood, where they have a virtual monopoly of the information and meanings the child receives concerning the recognisable fact that her skin is of a different colour to that of the majority of people she sees around her. Even into adolescence parents will continue to have significant control over the child's experience of her colour.

Broadly speaking, there are two ways in which this happens. First, parents control the amount of contact the child has with black people. For instance, in a society in which the black community is located in specific geographic areas, by the straightforward act of deciding where to live parents can have a crucial effect on their child's experience of her colour. Second, parents control the kind of information the child receives about her racial origins and how her different colour is defined. Definitions of race may range from its being literally 'skin-deep' to the child being the inheritor of a culture and racial identity which is and should be a crucial determinant of how she experiences the world.

Contact with the black community

We have already shown that the majority of the 36 families were living in areas which were either entirely white or in which there was only a small

Table 6.1 Number of black friends of the family

Number of black friends	Number of couples/ single parents
No black friends	18
1	7
2	4
3	0
4	0
5–9	3
10 or more	3
Total	35

proportion of black residents. In the interviews with the parents we explored in further detail their contact with black people.

We asked the parents, 'Do you have any close or relatively close friends who are not white?' In one of the couples that had separated, the father (who was caring for the child) said he had no friends who were black, whilst the mother answered that she had '10 or more'. But for the remainder there was consistency between the replies of parents where both were interviewed. Results are shown in Table 6.1.

These responses show that contact with black people either did not occur or was limited. The majority of families (32 out of 36) went further and said that being a mixed-race family had no effect on their choice of friends.

In the interviews we also asked, 'Has adopting . . . (child's name) affected where you live?' Replies indicated that in the majority of families (31 out of 36) having an adopted child of a different racial background had not been a significant factor in the decision.

None of the three couples who said that having adopted their child had been a significant factor in deciding where to live had moved house because they wanted to have more contact with racially-mixed communities:

> *Father:* Where we lived before . . . in a council flat at that time. And first of all the flat wasn't big enough and secondly we decided that if we were going to have children, it was best to have a home with a garden . . . On top of that, there was at that time a lot of Indian and Pakistani people moving into the . . . area which was creating quite a difficult colour problem. There was a lot of prejudice and feeling against coloured people. There still is in that area . . . so we moved out.

And:

> *Mother:* Yes, it did, actually. Definitely . . . (the area we lived in) was a pretty rough area. There were the odd remarks like 'wonder who her husband was'. It didn't worry me at all, but I thought this child is going to have enough problems without me forcing extra problems onto her just because I have chosen to live in a rough area. That was one reason why I moved here. I didn't want her to be subjected to anything like that.

The families in our group are largely middle class and houseowners and, irrespective of the perceived needs of their children, this is likely to be the main determining factor in where they live. Their position in the housing market makes it probable that they will live far away from the black areas of the inner cities. But we felt it important to follow up the issue of residential location and later in the interview asked the question, 'Do you think that in general it is easier for white parents to bring up a black/brown child in a white community or a racially-mixed one?' One couple gave different

59

responses, the mother saying that it was 'easier in a white community' and the father saying he 'did not know'. The answers of the remaining 35 couples were consistent:

Table 6.2 Where to live: parents' views

	Number of couples/ single parents
Easier in white community	14
Makes no difference	3
Easier in racially-mixed community	9
Other	.
	8
Impossible to code	
Don't know	1
Total	35

The responses to this question are less clear-cut than would be expected from previous answers, indicating perhaps that in view of the experiences of these families the question was more hypothetical than based on actual experience. It is, however, interesting to illustrate answers given in the two largest categories of response. Some parents thought it was 'easier in a white community':

Mother: We haven't tried it in a mixed-raced community. But I think perhaps it is more difficult. We've had no problems at all here, because there is no social friction here.
Father: Social friction of a racial nature must start when the numbers are . . . And that doesn't occur (here).

And:

Father: With a very pretty, not very dark, Indian girl probably easier in a white community. Early on. Later on, it doesn't make much difference . . . it's an interesting question . . . I would have thought that it's obvious that if there are general difficulties in the community because of a large proportion of coloured people, then it's going to be reflected on all the coloured people, including the adopted.

Others thought that it would be 'easier in a racially-mixed community':

Mother: Each community is so different. Each one has its own personality. I think on the whole (it would be easier) in a racially-mixed community, but there again, they're more likely to come up against prejudice, but I think they're more readily accepted as normal. One dark face where all other faces are white, well, they might be spoilt or they might be treated as a freak. I think a mixed community on the whole is easier, although it has its own problems.

And:

> *Father:* I think a racially-mixed one. I think it has been helpful to us that we live in a town where coloured faces are a frequent sight. Because when we do go on holidays to places where they are obviously a rare thing, then I certainly have been aware of — just people looking at us.

This last quote is of interest because it illustrates the latitude with which the term 'mixed-race community' is defined. The family in question live in a primarily white middle-class housing area and yet the town as a whole has a fairly high black population. This variety in the possible types of racially-mixed areas is also illustrated by the answer of another father who lived in a middle-class, but fairly cosmopolitan, area:

> *Father:* I would have said definitely easier in a racially mixed one . . . If you are talking about this kind of community, then I'm sure it is easier than living in a totally white community. I'm sure because the child just blends in. But if you're talking about a poverty-stricken area which is inhabited by poor people of a different ethnic background, then I suppose it could be a lot worse . . . But . . . I mean what you're looking for is our own personal experience . . . I'm afraid we can only talk from this rather middle-class sort of life that we live.

To sum up, most of the project families had only limited contact with the black community. Most lived in predominantly white areas, had few if any black friends and had not chosen where to live on the strength of their being a mixed-race family. There was no clear consensus among the families as to whether it was easier or more appropriate to bring up an adopted black or coloured child in a racially-mixed area. Indeed, if anything, the balance of opinion seems to have been that there were fewer problems associated with bringing up a black child in a white area than in a racially-mixed one. And fairly central to the parents' view of this was that in a racially-mixed area there was likely to be 'friction' and 'tension' and this friction or tension would have obvious implications for the child.

Affecting family life

We also asked a number of questions about whether having adopted a child of a different racial background had affected the family in its external relations. Again, the picture that emerges is that having adopted transracially had not had or been allowed to have a dramatic effect. For instance, the

61

parents of 31 of the children said it had made no difference to 'how they got on with close relatives'. The parents of 32 of the children said that 'it had made no difference to how neighbours reacted to them'. The parents of all 36 of the children said it made no differences in the family's ability to make friends.

We also asked the parents whether they had 'ever experienced hostility or aggression because of adopting a child of a different racial background'. The parents of 12 of the study children answered that they had. All of these indicated that this had been some years previously, and the descriptions that the parents gave in almost all cases referred to when the study child was very young. For instance, one mother told us:

> Mm. Yes, but not from immediate — you know, you find things. I remember we were at a picnic once . . . We'd only — . . . (study child) was little — we'd only had him for about a year and he was being really beastly. I gave him a really good slap on his leg and a woman actually came over and said to me, she said, 'That's the trouble with you people,' she said, 'You only have these children for the money'. You know. She said, 'You don't even look after them properly'.

And another told us:

> Yeah. Very, very early on when, when he was, when he was a tiny baby. Um, just occasionally, you know, you get people saying . . . (and) . . . sort of writ large all over, you know, all over their faces was sort of, I was sleeping, sleeping around with black men kind of syndrome.

Policies relating to racial identity

The second way in which parents of transracially-adopted children can control their children's experience of their colour is through the definitions of their racial background which are offered to them, whether they encourage them to identify with people of similar racial background and whether they introduce into the child's world knowledge, information and experiences relating to racial background.

We explored these issues in detail with the parents. The length of some of the replies and the care with which policies and experiences were described indicated that, at least in the early years, this was something that all the parents had thought about and in the majority of cases had come to develop relatively clear policies on.

First, we asked whether they felt it best to give the child a sense of identity with his/her racial background or to bring him/her up as a white child.

Table 6.3   Family policy towards racial background

	Number of couples or single parents answering in this way
Very positive attempt to give child pride in racial background	4
Some attempt to give child pride in racial background	13
No specific approach or bringing up child as entirely white child	19
Total	36

As was suggested in Chapter 2, it might be that white parents of mixed-race children take a significantly different approach to issues of racial identity than those of children neither of whose natural parents was white. There is, however, no clear evidence that this is the case. Of the four couples who had a positive approach to racial identity, two were the parents of mixed-race children. Of the 13 couples or single parents who made some attempt, five were the parents of mixed-race children.

The following is an example of a 'very positive attempt' to give their child a pride in racial background:

Mother: Because we've always believed in giving as much ethnic background to both of them as possible. As much as we can because we haven't been . . . to the West Indies or to Ghana. They know, if there's a programme on television, you know, they, we watch it together. A friend of ours has gone to Ghana and we asked him especially to bring something back for . . . (child's name) which he treasures actually very much. It seems to be the right thing . . . And we've always felt it really important not to call him a white child . . .

Thirteen couples made 'some attempt to give child pride in racial background'. For instance:

Mother: He's quite happy to learn English history and finds that very interesting, so I'd see this as a field where I really ought to find out something about Indian history, Indian culture. But the few efforts I've made haven't yielded anything that he's shown much interest in. The most recent one, I borrowed some books on Indian history from a family who have a son the same age as . . . (child's name) and gave these to . . . (child's name). So, OK, he looked at them and the

63

girls had a go through them as well and it was all very interesting. We gave them back, but he didn't want to follow it up or find some more. I was prepared to take him over to see what they'd got in . . . (the) library or anything like this, but he's never pushed for this so I've done no more about it and I shan't until something else crops up. When they were very small, I was quite glad to find those Oxfam books. Oxfam were beginning to get books published in India. Little Indian stories and one or two things like that, which, again, were treated just like any other story books, but at least they'd got coloured pictures in instead of white children in, and so on. But, again, only on a very casual basis.

Finally, the following are examples of how the largest group of parents responded, who were coded as 'no specific approach' or 'bringing up child entirely as white child'.

Father: Look, you can't bring them up anything, you know, than part of the thing that they are. You know, we wouldn't say, well, you know, on a Sunday morning, 'You'll have to go down to the Sikh temple because that's the way that, you know, your, your background goes'.

Mother: I think it's being as racialist as the people you condemn for being that because race is, it's, for a person in . . . (child's name) position, it's only a matter of personal appearance, it's only a matter of pigment in his skin. Someone in . . . (child's name) situation. I mean, if you try to bring him up as someone other than . . . I think if you are continually conscious of the child's race, you've never accepted the child as a person, have you?

Father: No.

Mother: I don't think about . . . (child's name) at all in that way.

Father: I think, you know, we would actively discourage him from thinking that way himself.

And:

Father: I think we tend to ignore it, you know. I mean we don't say he should be particularly proud or particularly ignore it.

Mother: He thinks . . .

Father: Pride in either way would to my mind just lead to problems anyway. Just, you know, he is what he is.

Mother: He identifies with both. I'm sure he is. He sees himself as being English because he says 'our King and Queen' and things like this, and 'isn't England a lovely country, Mummy?' and this, you know. He obviously belongs there, but he also, when he sees coloured people on television, especially dancing and singing and things like this, he identifies with them. He feels he belongs to them somehow, I'm sure he does.

The parents' answers help to illustrate some of the underlying problems they experienced in helping their children to develop an identity based on race.

First of all, there is the difficulty that a significant proportion of these children had natural parents of dissimilar racial backgrounds (see Chapter 3). How, then, should adoptive parents deal with the expectation that they should give the child an identity based on the racial background of natural parents? This point is best illustrated by the reply of one of the mothers:

in theory, yes, we agree very much with racial identity. In theory, I think it's, it's . . . the child's roots and all that. But, in practice, it's virtually impossible. I mean, because, you see, you take . . . (child's name), who was born in this country, fair enough. Her mother was a Kenyan Asian, who'd never seen India and only lived in Kenya, and her father was a West Indian — presumably his roots are back in Africa somewhere. And then you say, right, now you're going to give this child some kind of racial heritage and you just, really just don't know where to start. We've stuck more or less to India.

Added to this, there was the feeling on the part of some parents that to attempt to instil a racial identity was 'false' and not related to the realities of life as the child was experiencing them:

Mother: Well, I get the feeling that we know very little about the particular culture and background of . . . (child's name). I do feel sometimes that we ought to be concentrating on it a bit more, but we don't.
Father: Yes, except that the life she's leading now is not related to her cultural background, the culture of her background.
Mother: No.
Father: And it always strikes me as being a little bit artificial and bogus to contrive to do this in a self-conscious way. I think it only matters if she's interested in — like anyone else is interested in, you know — other cultures.

And:

Mother: I think it is really very difficult for a child brought up in a white, middle-class family in this sort of an area to identify with anything but that family and her whole life, her whole life is very absorbing and full of interests and that is her real life to her. Not some strange place somewhere else. That's the feeling that one has. Of course, she's travelled a bit and is likely to feel for different cultures.

Some of the parents pointed to what they considered to be the dangers of this approach: that the child would be given an identity which would have little support in the world as she experienced it. Added to which was the problem that by highlighting an alternative identity for the child, they were in fact introducing a distinction between the child and the rest of the family.

Mother: Yes, but I think it is — I, I say it's nice in theory, but it's difficult really to put it into practice. You seem to be making such a thing that they are different if you're not careful.

Reading the transcripts of what each of the parents said in answer to this question, two other points stand out clearly. First, some of the families had attempted to introduce to the child information about her racial background when the child had been younger, but because this had been met with a lack of interest, it had not been pursued. For instance, one couple told us:

Mother: We used to think the former, didn't we, when she was tiny? We used to think it was terribly important.

Father: Yes, I wrote to the Pakistan High Commission asking for all the bumf they could send and it's been around, but I don't think she's ever really bothered with it. She might have it in her bedroom.

Mother: I think it's keeping a balance that's important, really. You know, the awareness that the family you were born from, knowing what their culture was to some extent, but, I think it's very difficult for her because there, there's a conflict there, and she doesn't belong there, she doesn't belong with them, she doesn't belong to any Pakistani community here. So she's, she has some kind of a conflict, she must have. So I think it's keeping a balance.

And:

Mother: He doesn't seem to have an interest. He's never asked me anything about India. He seems to have no interest at all, and I've told him different things about his parents and he didn't seem at all interested, and I always hope that, you know, one day he'll be able to make a contact, but now I've changed my mind, you know. I think it's too late.

Again:

Mother: We don't actually think of her as coloured, do we, really? But, when they were younger, I used to find out things that were Indian . . . if they came on the television. But she's not really sort of shown a great deal of interest in that sort of thing.

Second, some of the parents were waiting for the child to take the initiative on the issue of racial identity and if the child was not making any moves in that direction, then all was presumed to be well. The following pieces of conversation from separate families illustrate this point:

Mother: Oh yes. I thought she'd lost interest because I found that whenever, if I brought up the subject, she didn't seem as though she wanted to talk about it . So I stopped talking about it and was waiting, really, for her to bring the subject up, but she hasn't spoken to me about it for a long time, and I don't believe in pushing it. But the extraordinary thing is, she can't stand the heat. I mean she can stand the heat less than we can.

And:

> *Father:* I wouldn't be at all surprised if at some point she really picked on Indian things and thought they were lovely, you know. But I wouldn't want to force it on her and I wouldn't want to sort of rub it in, you know. I just wonder whether it may emerge some time.
>
> *Mother:* Yes, in a way I wish it would sometimes because she would look so gorgeous in . . .
>
> *Father:* A sari, yes.
>
> *Mother:* The colours and everything. But, until she wants to or takes a pride in it . . .

The interviews seem, therefore, to support a picture of many of the parents having introduced information related to colour into the child's experience at earlier stages in their lives, but by the time the children reached adolescence this was seen as inappropriate, either because the parents see it as potentially causing difficulties for the child, or, more likely, because she is 'uninterested'.

This is supported by answers to another question which asked if the child had faced difficulties over 'colour' and when these difficulties had been most apparent. The parents of 12 children said the child had never faced difficulties and two did not know. Of the remaining 24, two said she had when she was under five years, five said between the ages of five and eight, 11 said between the ages of eight and 11, and four said from 11 years onwards.

The fact that the child's racial background is now perceived as less important is also borne out by answers to the question, 'Do you think more or less about (child)'s colour compared with when he/she was a young child (e.g., under five)?' Each parent was asked this question individually. Forty-one of the 70 parents interviewed thought about colour less than they had, 18 'about the same', and only three thought about it more. For six it had never been significant. The responses of two parents were impossible to code.

Racial background and life chances

The information presented so far in this chapter gives an idea of the approach that these parents were taking to their children's 'colour' or 'racial background' and of some of the difficulties that were perceived as inherent in offering the children an identity which is likely to distinguish them from members of the immediate family and those they meet in their social world outside the family.

Underpinning the majority approach of not highlighting the child's racial background appears to have been a conception that the child's colour was not necessarily significant in determining life chances. Listening to the recorded interviews from the parents, we were struck by the frequency with which parents made such remarks as, 'Yes, her colour would be a problem if it weren't for her personality/ability to get on with people/academic achievements/ambition to succeed'.

Some systematic information on this was produced by the responses to two questions. First, we asked the parents, 'Many people would agree that West Indian/Asian children in this country face a lot of problems. Would you agree?'. All of the 36 couples or single parents agreed with this view-point, and in their answers reference was made to a wide range of dis-advantages, including discrimination from the police, difficulties in the job market, difficulties at school, and 'culture conflict'.

We then asked, 'Does . . . (child's name) experience these?' Twenty-four answered that their child did not face similar problems, compared with seven couples who felt that she did. A further four felt that similar problems might arise in the future. One response was impossible to code. From these answers it is clear that the majority of the parents perceived their children as not facing similar problems to black children growing up with black parents: or, put another way, that growing up in their present families gave the child the opportunity to avoid the disadvantages of racial background.

> *Mother:* I don't think she can (face these problems) because she has been brought up as an English family. One of the teachers commented once that between . . . (child's name) and the Kenyan Asians that had come over — she was the first person that had put it into words for me — that the cultural differences between those children and . . . (child's name) were tremendous . . . (child's name) just happens to have a darker skin and different colouring.

And:

> *Father:* I don't think . . . (child's name) does because without wanting to sound pompous, I think she's rather privileged . . . Hopefully, by the time she goes out into the world, she's going to have a degree or something or other and won't face those sorts of problems.

It is, however, worth noting that in replies to this question, the issue of mixed racial background comes up as an advantage. For instance, one father,

68

after talking about difficulties experienced by black people in getting jobs, said:

> *Father:* I don't think, to be quite honest, I don't think he will because if he was completely black, I think he would do. But . . . (child's name) isn't. That makes a different impression on employers. I think it's the depth of colour that has an impression on an employer. I really do. I think if someone is completely black, a little bit of prejudice comes up. But they get someone like . . . (child's name), a goldeny colour, they tend to bypass that.

However, somewhat inconsistent with the results of the above question were the answers to an earlier question: 'Would you say that . . . (child's name) needs to do better at school than a white child to have the same chances in life?' At least one member of 15 couples said 'yes'; 20 couples said 'no', and one was undecided.

It is impossible to give a definite reason for this inconsistency of more parents saying the child had 'to do better at school' than saying that they 'faced similar problems'. Perhaps one reason is that, although the parents did not see their children as suffering from the deprived living standards and general discrimination that afflict many black people, some did see racial background as significant when it came to looking for jobs, even middle-class jobs, and that it was therefore necessary for the child to be armed with better qualifications.

Summary

In this chapter we have explored the approach taken by the parents to their children's different racial background and the perceptions of racial background that have guided their approach. This has been done because one of the central social work approaches to transracial placement has been that it is essential that the child should develop an identity which incorporates a very positive view of her racial background. Also, as we argued at the beginning of the chapter, it is the parents who are crucial in determining their children's experience of colour.

Summarising the information presented in this chapter, it is clear that the majority of these parents were not highlighting and focusing upon their children's racial background. There is some evidence that in the past, when the children were younger, some of the parents had made considerable efforts in this direction, but now that the children have reached their teens, this does not appear to be a matter of primary concern to the majority of these families.

It is, of course, easy to be critical of this approach. One could argue that the parents were 'laundering' their children and were denying them access to their racial heritage. However, listening to the parents talking we have been struck by the way in which they have had to face what could be called the central paradox of transracial placement. This paradox can be stated in the following way. The parents are encouraged to support and emphasise the 'differentness' of their children. At the same time, as adoptive parents, they see one of their main tasks as making the children feel an integral part of their family.

Given this paradox and its contradictory pressures, it is perhaps not surprising that the majority of these parents have opted for an approach which does not involve attempting to make the children appear different and which has meant that complex and difficult issues such as 'racial heritage' and 'racial identity' have been changed to much more manageable issues of 'colour'. It must also be remembered that these parents adopted their children at a time when *not* highlighting their child's racial background was regarded as the appropriate approach. The way in which they are bringing up their children seems consistent with the 'melting pot' approach of the 1960s.

7

The child's conception of racial background

In the last chapter we began to tackle one of the central issues of transracial adoption — the meaning of race within the family. We showed that the majority of children were being brought up in families in which the parents did not offer them an identity which emphasised their racial background. If this is the case, what then of the children? Central to the previous writing on transracial adoption is that without such a sense of racial identity the child will face difficulties. The critics of transracial adoption have argued that the child will not know who she is. Particularly as adolescence approaches she will come to face identity conflict and confusion. It will be at this age that the child becomes fully aware of the social meanings given to 'blackness' and 'whiteness'. Unable to relate positively to her racial background she will take on the stigmatizing white perceptions of her origins.

Studying 'identity conflict' in transracially-adopted adolescents produces a number of difficulties. First, the term is used in the literature in a pejorative way. A conflict in identity is seen as pathological rather than possibly offering the scope for creative development. Second, like the related term of 'culture conflict', it tends to be used in a loose and ill-defined way. Where exactly in the child's experience of the world is the conflict located and how significant is it? Third, the use of the term in relation to transracially-adopted children would seem to presume that such children have available for them in their daily lives two identities: that of a white child or that of a black child. At the very least it presumes that transracially-adopted children have available for them information and knowledge about an alternative lifestyle and mode of being which is consistent with their racial background. Because of mixed schooling and mixed residential areas the black child growing up in the black community is likely in this society to be familiar with white identity models: the same, however, cannot necessarily be said about black children growing up in white families. Their experience, as has already been suggested in this study, may be entirely white.

As far as the third difficulty is concerned, the challenge would seem to be to get at the particular experiences and feelings of these children in relation to their racial origins without necessarily presuming that they have alternative identity models. We must attempt to get the children to explain to us

71

how they see themselves in terms of racial background and through their words assess whether their lives in this area are significantly problematic. Such a task is consistent with Weinrich's general requirement that

> an explanation of how the individual comes to change the meaning of group membership for himself must use theoretical concepts that define his ethnic identifications in his own terms.[1]

It is also consistent with recent work on the children of mixed marriages which has recognised the complexity of the child's conception of race and that the child need not necessarily see racial background in 'black and white' terms. Wilson argues that

> in the street, the home and the playground it is often necessary for a child to recognise and juggle with all the different characteristics which go to make up 'race'. How I look, speak, dress, dance, do my hair, what music and food I like, what stereotypes I hold about my own and other groups' . . . whiteness or non-whiteness may still be the main message the child receives from society, but in everyday life all children have to deal with a more complex categorisation and pecking order than this.[2]

What we have attempted to do, therefore, in this chapter is to build up a picture of how the children experience and feel about their racial background. In doing this we have used a number of approaches. First, we present the results of questions aimed at getting a general picture of how the children perceive themselves: we asked them what they look like, what vocabulary they use to describe their racial background, what they know about people of similar racial background to themselves and whether they perceive themselves as being similar. Second, we consider their orientation towards their racial background: whether they are 'proud' of their racial origins, whether in the future they would like more contact with people of similar racial origins and whether they would like to 'live like' people of similar racial background.

In the analysis that follows we have also, where the results warrant it, drawn the distinction between the mixed-race children and the children of whom both the natural parents were black. This has been necessary because there may well be differences in how these children perceive themselves in terms of racial background.

Racial origins and self-perception

Appearance
To get the children to describe how they perceive their physical appear-

ance, we asked them, 'Imagine someone is meeting you at a train station who has never seen you before. How would you describe what you look like?' Of the 36 children, 23, without any interviewer prompting, referred to their colour. Eleven of these were boys and 12 were girls. Ten of the 23 were mixed race. There is thus little evidence that the mixed-race children were generally less likely to perceive themselves as 'coloured'. The following responses are typical:

Boy: I'd probably say I've got black hair, but loads of people have black hair, or, mmm . . . I'd probably say, well, I'd probably say I'd be walking down with a coat on. No, I wouldn't say that because lots of people have coats on. Oh dear, I don't see . . . so how I would look? Probably fairly short, probably tell them the size of my, how long my hair is and probably say, like, my colour, and probably seeing me they would have known. Tell them what type of clothes I was wearing if I had, if I was still wearing the same ones then.

Girl: Well, I'm quite easy to spot because I'm half-Ghanaian. I've got dark black curly hair; fairly tall; brown skin — and I'd probably be waving madly!

Boy: Well, of course, I'm coloured, aren't I? That should distinguish me. Average height — average in everything really, average size. Um, well, quite smart appearance usually if I'm meeting somebody.

Interestingly, some of the children referred to their colour, but qualified it by saying it was only 'slight'. For instance:

Boy: Well, I've got black hair; slightly, um, light brown skin; um, about five foot eight, I should think; not fat, but I'm not thin either; um, I've got brown eyes.

Girl: Oh, I see. Say — I'm five foot whatever, tallish, something like that. Say what, say what sort of clothes I'd wear, be wearing — coat or something. And that I was slightly dark-skinned and — I don't know.

The remaining 13 made no reference to colour, although one girl described herself as having a 'dark complexion'. Also, one mixed-race girl made a point of saying she was 'white':

Girl: I don't know. I think . . . I know. I suppose I'd describe what my hair looks like. I'd probably make a point of wearing my hair in a special way as well, you know. She'd know, you know, how to find me in that sort of sense, but — I don't know. I suppose, I'd describe myself as medium-height, I mean, you know. I don't know — I can't think of anything else that I could sort of say. Well, I suppose I could say I was white and, you know — that's the other thing. But I can't think of anything else.

These descriptions give insights into how the children see their physical appearance, but, as with all such data, it is necessary to be a little wary in interpretation. However, it seems that a significant majority of the children correctly described themselves as looking 'coloured' and regarded this as a significant aspect of their appearance. Whether the remaining children were avoiding descriptions of themselves in terms of colour, incorrectly perceived themselves as 'looking white' or thought there were other things more important (hair style, clothes, etc.) is impossible to tell.

Words in use

The way in which families and individuals talk about racial origins is an important indication of their perceptions and definitions of this aspect of their background. We asked the children, 'Would you call yourself coloured, black, brown, West Indian/Indian or do you use another description?' Of the 36 children, nine said that there was no description in regular use and the response of one child was impossible to code. Of the nine children, only three were of mixed natural parentage. Responses for the remaining 26 were as follows:

Table 7.1 Terms used by children to describe themselves

'Brown'	11
'Coloured'	8
'English'/'British'	2
'Dark'	2
'Indian'	1
'Pale brown or yellow'	1
'Slightly dark-skinned and Italian'	1
Total	26

The responses to this question, apart from indicating that a sizeable number of the children had no regular vocabulary for describing racial origins, also indicates that none of the children used the term 'black' to describe themselves. The most common words in use were 'brown' and 'coloured'.[3] Table 7.1 also shows that only one boy referred to himself in more specific racial terms (i.e., 'Indian'). Also of interest is the last response in the table. The girl in question was part-West Indian and yet lived in an area in which the largest racial minority group was Italian. To describe herself as 'slightly dark-skinned and Italian' is a nice example of the way in which young people adapt to the social surroundings in which they find themselves.

Perceptions of being 'like' other black children

To understand the self-perception of transracially-adopted children we felt it was crucial to establish whether they considered themselves to be similar to black children growing up in black families. Before doing this we had to assess what information and knowledge they had about such children and more generally about the culture of one or both of their natural parents.

First, we asked, 'Are you interested in finding out about West Indian/Asian life?' (i.e., the cultural life of one or both of their natural parents). Only 13 of the 36 children answered that they were. A disproportionate eight of the 13 were boys; six were of mixed-race parentage.

We then asked the 13 'interested' children where and from whom they 'learnt' about 'West Indian/Asian' life. The most common sources were television (ten), books (eight), and adoptive parents (six).

We then asked, 'Can you describe a typical West Indian/Asian boy or girl growing up in a West Indian/Asian family in this country? What is he/she like as a person and how does he/she spend his/her time?'. Twenty-one of the children were able to give a reply; 15 could not.

Only a minority of the 21 children who were able to give replies were able to talk about specific contact with black adolescents:

Boy: I don't really know. I don't much from what I've heard about or seen about . . . There was, you know, this boy in my old school. I learnt à bit just by surmising — I don't know whether that's the right word . . . You know, I just sort of, I saw him and I saw his brothers and the type of person he was. I mean, if we were all right over in the far corner of the field and told your friend, 'Get some ice-cream, will ya'. And he'd go, 'Get out. You go and get it yourself'. If you asked . . . (boy's name), he'd get it for you. That sort of thing, you know. He was very sort of quiet, nice, but people abused him because he was coloured, because he was Hindu and because he had a turban.
I think he gets on, he's part of the community, of the Indian family living here, you know. First of all, he had that little, sort of handkerchief on his head, and when he came to school again after the summer holidays, he had a big black turban. He looked sort of grand in that. I mean, I could appreciate that they look good on people, although other people don't.

And:

Girl: Well, my friends . . . they're sisters. They were brought over from Asia to come to England and they know an awful lot and they tell me about . . .
Interviewer: Do you go to their homes?
Girl: No. I'm not allowed in because I'm half-English. I think it's in Indian families that a young, uh, if a young Indian and an English person or any other nationality . . . has a baby, then it's a disgrace upon them and, see, I'm not allowed in the, the sort of family house.

Interviewer: I see. Who's told you this? Has . . . (friend's name) told you this?

Girl: Yes. She was very embarrassed about it. I felt really sorry. It's her father really, you know. He's very strict.

Most gave responses based on very limited contact:

Girl: No. But I've seen, um, quite a few Indian families. Not, I've never seen the houses, I don't think, except for in London perhaps. A place where a lot of them are. But I've seen quite a few people, um, in, the ladies in, um, — what are they called — saris. I've seen a lot of people in those and, um, I don't, I don't know anyone. You know, I've never seen anyone. There tend to be a lot more people in London.

Interviewer: D'you know what sort of life they lead? D'you know what sort of things they do?

Girl: Ah. Something's just flashed. I think. Yes. Where my auntie . . . lives in London, she, there's this wine shop, which, um, um, an Indian couple work, um — you know, they keep, it's theirs, you know, they keep it — and, um, they, the lady and the man, they both dress like Indians really, you know. Um. They don't seem any different, really, they're — I remember once I went to get a bottle of something for . . . (aunt) and I couldn't quite hear her because she had a funny accent. But I, no, I've no idea of how they live.

The most striking aspect of these responses is that at least 12 of the 21 children who could give a reply talked about the difficulties and problems of being a 'typical West Indian/Asian boy or girl growing up in a West Indian/Asian family in this country'. Some of these talked about the general difficulties of being black in a white society. For instance, one boy told us:

Boy: In London there's racial conflict and all the black kids keep together, don't mix about very much, they're always afraid what's going to happen.

Interviewer: So, d'you think you'd have had a different character if you'd been brought up in those circumstances?

Boy: I'd probably have been a bit harder, you know. Stand on my own feet a bit more.

And another boy told us, perhaps not entirely forgetting his own experience:

Boy: Oh, I think at the start it'd be a very hard life because he's got to get used to other people who would not really be taking to him, black fellows. But once he gets settled with them and people start to take to him, he's got to make himself be liked by other people and he's got to make friends quickly, and once he's got friends, I think he'll get along very quickly.

But the most commonly mentioned difficulty was the 'strictness' of the upbringing that their counterparts would experience:

76

Girl: They're very religious, I think, and fixed marriages and things like that and very strict upbringing.

And:

Girl: A Pakistani kind of life. She wouldn't be allowed to go out much, socialise. She wouldn't be, mix with boys, I suppose, and she'd have to do more or less what her parents told her because they're very strict and that's all I know, really. Well, they'd have to help their mother a lot, and, um, they wouldn't be allowed out much. Um, they wouldn't be allowed boyfriends other than their own race, and they'd have to wear a sari.

After we had asked the children to describe a typical counterpart of theirs, we asked the 21 children who could give a description, 'How do you and your life compare with the description you have just given?' The children were asked to tick boxes and the results were as follows: three answered 'only different in a few ways or no differences', four answered 'different in some ways, not in others', and 14 answered 'very different or different in most ways'.

We then asked, 'What are the main problems that face West Indian/Asian boys/girls of your age growing up in West Indian/Asian families in this country?' Only four of the children were unable to give answers to this question, indicating that more of the children were aware of 'problems' than differences in lifestyle and personality.

A wide range of problems was referred to, including language difficulties, the National Front, relations being unable to join them, poor living standards, no freedom because of religious beliefs. Because some children referred to several 'problems' it is difficult to break down replies into subject categories, but the following are representative:

Boy: Well, getting a job and National Front and all that.
Girl: Lack of money because their parents haven't had very good education, so when they don't have good jobs they wouldn't have very much money. Um, people like the National Front always doing marches and things. I don't think they'd have *that* many problems, really. They usually seem to be quite friendly people.
Boy: Sort of like immigration things and that sort of thing. And having their, and trying, trying to get their fathers and that lot over here. Can't come over.
Girl: I suppose people would mock them, their religion and appearance and the clothes they have to wear.
Girl: Well, if a boy wanted to go out with them, they'd have to say, no, wouldn't they?
Girl: Oh, um, probably the prejudice of other people. Um, that sort of thing, I

77

mean. Um. Language problems and, um, religion problems. If they were still Hindus or something like that, might find it difficult.

In at least one of the responses there is evidence of the child in part referring to his own experiences:

> *Boy:* Troubles at school. If you're in a place where there are a lot of coloured people, you're all right. If not, you've got to get a firm grip. If you don't get that firm grip or anything like it, you can slip and everybody will just get on to you, which is what happened about six months ago. I'm not particularly strong — strong in words, but that doesn't matter, I'm just not strong. I've never tried fighting out of anything. Wording, yes. I can word my way round anything, but I can't fight because I just don't like fighting.

Where appropriate we asked whether the child faced similar problems. Of the 30 replies, only four children (including three boys) felt their problems were completely or mostly the same as those faced by West Indian/Asian boys and girls growing up in West Indian/Asian communities in this country; six (including five boys) felt they were the same in some ways, but not in others. A large group of 16 felt their problems were 'mostly different' or completely different, and other replies were inconclusive.

These responses show that there were marginally more children who perceived themselves as having similar problems to black children in black families than saw themselves as being similar to and as leading similar lives to black children in black families. But again more children saw themselves not facing these problems than facing them. The other interesting point about this result is that boys seemed to be very disproportionately represented in terms of seeing themselves facing similar problems.

Orientation to racial origins

Three questions were aimed at getting at the children's emotional orientations towards their racial background. First, we asked which of the following statements 'fits how you really feel': (a) I am proud to be coloured/black/brown; (b) I don't really mind what colour I am; (c) I would prefer to be white. The children were asked to tick one of these statements. One girl said she couldn't put a tick in only one box because most of the time she didn't really mind what colour she was, but sometimes she would 'prefer to be white'. Results for the remaining 35 children are in Table 7.2.

These results seem to indicate that only a small minority of the children had positive feelings about their racial backgrounds. However, it is interesting to note that two of the five children who were proud to be 'coloured' were of mixed racial background.

It is interesting to compare the findings on this question with the parents'

Table 7.2 Children's attitudes to their colour

Statements	Boys	Girls	Total
I am proud to be coloured/black/brown	1	4	5
I don't really mind what colour I am	10	13	23
I would prefer to be white	3	4	7
Totals	14	21	35

policy on racial identity and 'pride'. Of the five children who were 'proud', three had parents either or both of whom we had coded as making 'some attempt to give child pride in racial background'. Of the seven children who said they would 'prefer to be white', five parents were coded as having either no specific approach on 'pride' or as attempting to bring up their child 'entirely as a white child'. The numbers are obviously too small for tests of statistical significance, but the results do suggest a relationship between children's 'pride' and parental approach.

Towards the end of the interview we also asked the children two questions about whether they would develop links with their 'own' racial communities in the future.[4] In reply, 30 of the 36 children felt that when they were older and left home they would *not* like to live in the same way as West Indian or Asian people; only two felt that they would. Some offered an explanation:

Girl: No. I don't think I could because I've been brought up in England.
Boy: I think I've become too much separated from that style. I would like to know more about them when I am older and I would appreciate that I am one of those in a sense, but I wouldn't go back to living like . . .
Girl: I wouldn't fit with the way they live; I wouldn't be able to fit . . . . I wouldn't be known.
Girl: Um, well, most black families seem to be quite disorganised, really. I wouldn't like to have a disorganised family or anything like that, but I don't really know how they live, so . . .
Girl: Well, definitely not like in Africa because I think it's too hot out there. They don't have so nice homes and things like that, and in England, they're still a bit poor here — I wouldn't really like to live like most of them do.

We also asked the children the related question, 'When you are older and leave home would you like to spend time with West Indian/Asian people?' Five of the children answered in a way that was impossible to code. Of the remaining 31, 20 said 'no', nine said 'yes' and two were uncertain. There seems no clear relationship between mixed-race parentage and responses to this question. Three of the nine who answered 'yes' were mixed-race and 11 of the 20 who answered 'no' were mixed-race. Rather more therefore, but still a minority, of the children (nine out of 31) wanted to 'spend time with West Indian/Asian people' when they were older and left home. One of the boys told us:

> *Boy:* Oh, I'd spend some time with them. I'd just carry on as before, you know, except get to meet more coloured people.

But the majority did not:

> *Boy:* No, not really, because I have never experienced their sort of life style anyway because I am not really interested.

And:

> *Boy:* I've never sort of mixed with coloured people before. All my friends have, sort of, been white.

And the following is an example of one of the ones it was impossible to code:

> *Girl:* Not really bothered one way or the other, whoever I like best. If I met a friend who was white, I'd still be friends with them, and if I met a friend who was black, I'd still be friends with them.

Summary

In this chapter we have presented our findings on the children's self-conception in relation to their racial background. Obviously, no entirely consistent picture emerges, and some children are more interested in, knowledgeable about and orientated towards their racial origins. However, the majority of children share a very similar range of attitudes and perceptions.

The majority of the BAP children defined themselves as 'looking' coloured and saw this as a significant aspect of their appearance. Their self-perceptions in this sense were accurate. The vocabulary they used to describe themselves in terms of racial background tended to be non-specific in the sense that they did not link their racial origins with a particular racial group. Most were either 'coloured' or 'brown'; the term 'black' was not used.

Knowledge of their counterparts growing up in black families was limited and the majority of the children saw their lives as being dissimilar from the

lives of such children. In particular, they defined the lives of their counterparts in black families as being problematic in ways that they avoided by
being part of a white family.

There is little evidence of positive pride in racial background. Few of the
children wanted to 'live like' their own race counterparts in the future,
although a somewhat larger number indicated the desire to have contact
with such groups.

There is no clear evidence of a relationship between mixed-race parentage
and orientation towards racial background.

The evidence from this chapter paints a picture of children who, although
not directly denying their racial background, perceived themselves to be
'white' in all but skin colour. Their lives were different and their anticipations about the future were different. There was little evidence of a positive
sense of racial identity. In this our data supports those critics of transracial
adoption who have seen this as being a likely outcome and one of its major
dangers.

8

Difficulties in the children's lives

A central criticism of transracial adoption is that the children will face major difficulties in their lives. Being black in a white family will be experienced as problematic and will be associated with a feeling of confusion about themselves which will be reflected in low self-esteem and possibly in the development of behavioural problems. To test this we used a number of approaches. First, we carried out standardised self-esteem tests with the children; second, we asked parents and teachers to fill out standardised scales relating to behavioural disorder — the Rutter scales A and B. Third, and consistent with the general approach of the study, we asked the children to discuss with us directly their 'feelings' about being black in a white family.

Self-esteem

The Coopersmith self-esteem inventory[1] involves the children saying whether a statement is true or false in relation to themselves. Children are presented with 58 statements, such as 'I'm pretty sure of myself', 'I'm good fun to be with', 'I'm proud of my school work', 'No one pays much attention to me at home', 'I have a low opinion of myself' and they have to tick whether the statement is true or false for them. They are told to try to tick whether the statement is true or false in their case, but if it is really necessary, they are told they can say they are 'uncertain'.

We used a version of the Coopersmith inventory that was also used by Holbrook[2] in a recent study of children's self-perceptions in different types of family situation. This version only involves minor modifications to the original, converting to English from American usage.

Incorporated into the Coopersmith inventory are eight 'lie' questions, such as 'I like everyone I know', 'I'm never unhappy'. If the children respond repeatedly in the affirmative to such statements, doubts arise about the validity of their other responses.

The number of children answering in the affirmative to each of the 'lie' statements was as follows:

82

I never worry about anything	0
I always do the right thing	0
I'm never unhappy	5
I like everyone I know	16
I never get scolded	3
I'm never shy	6
I always tell the truth	8
I always know what to say to people	6

Four children each replied 'yes' to four of these statements; most children only gave a 'yes' response to one of the 'lie' questions. We are therefore fairly confident that the great majority of the children were attempting to give an accurate representation of their feelings. At the end of the analysis that follows we do, however, indicate the differences that discounting this group of four children would have made.

Scoring for the Coopersmith test is as follows. Responses indicating positive self-esteem are scored as 2, responses indicating negative self-esteem are scored as 0. Responses of 'uncertain' are scored as 1. From the 50 items on the scale (i.e., excluding the eight lie statements), a child can score a maximum of 100 (high self-esteem) and a minimum of 0 (low self-esteem).

The 36 children in our group had a mean score on this inventory of 79 (range 49–100). The mean score for girls was 81 (range 56–100), and for boys, 77 (range 49–93). If we exclude the four children (3 girls, 1 boy) with the high 'lie' scores, the overall mean is marginally reduced to 78.

The results for our children give little indication of low self-esteem. This becomes particularly apparent when our results are put against those of the other studies which have used the same inventory. Holbrook administered the test to 20 foster-children, 20 adopted children and a control group of 20 children living with their natural parents. The age-range of her children was somewhat lower than ours (10–13 years), but according to Coopersmith the test results remain relatively consistent during this period.[3] Holbrook's figures were a mean score of 61 for the foster-children, a mean score of 69 for children in biological families, and of 73 for the adopted children.

At a different stage of the interview we also asked the children to complete another self-esteem scale, derived from the original Rosenberg scale.[4] Rosenberg used 10 statements related to conception of self with four possible ways for the child to respond (strongly agree, agree, disagree, strongly disagree).

In using the Rosenberg scale we followed the modifications suggested by Louden in his work with West Indian adolescents[5] and on the basis of pilot interviews we also found it necessary to make several further modifications.[6]

In the table below we present the results obtained with the 36 children using this modified scale. For the purposes of analysis and presentation we have combined responses of 'strongly agree' with 'agree' and also 'strongly disagree' with 'disagree'.

Table 8.1   Children's self-esteem: Rosenberg scale

Statements	No. saying 'true'	No. uncertain	No. saying 'false'
I am a person at least equal with others	32	1	3
I have a number of good qualities	31	2	3
I don't care what happens to me	1	0	35
I am able to do things as well as most other people	35	1	0
I do not have much to be proud of	6	0	30
On the whole I am satisfied with myself	32	0	4
Things are all mixed up in my life	4	0	32
Sometimes I think I am no good at all	14	1	21

The results shown in Table 8.1 give little support to the notion that the study children devalue themselves and have a low self-esteem. As many as 13 indicated positive self-esteem on all eight items; 13 others failed to indicate positive self-esteem in only one of the eight statements. Only two of the children (both boys) responded negatively to half or more of the statements. It is also significant that by far the highest number of responses that would apparently indicate low self-esteem were to the statement, 'Sometimes I think I am no good at all'. It may well be that such feelings are common to a majority of children as they pass through adolescence.

Both of these tests, therefore, indicate positive self-esteem amongst the study children. This conclusion is reinforced by the high degree of consistency between the two tests in relation to our group. The two boys who scored lowest on the Rosenberg/Louden scale also were two of the three lowest scorers on the Coopersmith test. On the basis of a comparison with the Holbrook group it is also tempting to conclude that the results are even higher than for other groups. However, the purpose of using these inventories was not for us to be able to draw fine comparisons between transracially adopted children and children in other types of family situation. Given the inherent difficulties of accurately assessing adolescent self-esteem, this would perhaps be unwise. Our purpose has been less ambitious — to see whether there is any evidence of a general lack of positive self-esteem in the group of children we talked to. Although several of our group came out relatively low on the self-esteem scales, we must conclude from the results on the Coopersmith scale and the Rosenberg/Louden scale that we can find no evidence to suggest that our group has a lack of a sense of self-esteem.

The Rutter scales

If the study children were experiencing undue difficulties in their lives, we might expect that there would be a significant degree of behavioural difficulty. To examine this we asked the parents to complete the Rutter scale A2 and the teachers who knew the children best to fill in the Rutter scale B2.[7]

The parents' scale consists of 31 brief statements concerning the child's behaviour. The parent is asked to indicate the frequency of occurrence of the behaviour, or the degree of its severity or the extent to which the statement applies to the child. Each item is scored 0, 1 or 2, producing a total score within the range 0–62. For the Rutter A2 scale the children who gain a total score of 13 or more are regarded as showing 'some disorder'.

Only three (two boys and one girl) of the 36 study children scored above 13 on this scale. The mean score on the scale for the 36 children was 5·72. These results appear generally consistent with the results obtained by Holbrook in the recent study already referred to. Of the 20 white adopted children in her sample, one came above the break point of 13. The mean score of the adopted children studied by Holbrook was 6·95.

The teachers' scale (scale B2) consists of 26 brief statements concerning the child's behaviour. The teacher has to indicate whether each statement applies to the child. The break point on this scale is nine, and four of the BAP children scored above this, indicating 'some disorder' from the perspective of the teacher.[8] It is perhaps a further indication of the validity of these two scales that all three children who indicated 'some disorder' on the parents' scale, also did so on the teachers' scale. The mean score of the BAP children on the Rutter B scale was 3·19.

Again, our purpose has not been to draw fine distinctions between the Rutter scale results of the BAP group and those of other tested groups. Rather, it has been to indicate if there is a significant degree of behavioural disorder within the group. On the basis of the findings presented above we conclude that there is not.

How it 'feels'

One of our main aims is to use the children's own words to describe themselves, their relationships and their lives. We therefore asked the children directly about one of the central issues of the research: 'Can you tell me how it feels being black/brown/coloured in a white family? Does it give you any problems or is it all straightforward?' We anticipated that if their position were regarded as problematic in terms of conflicting images of themselves or if their lives in a white family were regarded as particularly difficult because of their racial background, then responses to these questions would show this.

The coding was straightforward: 'problem/no problem'. It must, however, be noted that in some interviews the children had already touched on issues or 'problems' related to their racial origin. In such cases the interviewers referred back to these earlier statements or responses and asked them to expand on them. These prompted responses have been included in the 'problems' coding.

Of the 36 children coded, six responses indicated 'problems' (three boys and three girls; two were mixed-race). One girl was coded as 'problems, but in the past'. The remaining 29 children were recorded as having 'no problems'. Interestingly, the three lowest scorers on the Coopersmith scale were all in the group of six children whom we coded as having 'problems'.

First, three responses from representatives of the six children we coded as experiencing problems:

Boy: Yes, it gives me problems. But not so many that I get really upset. It's just the occasional problem where I've found I've got to start explaining it to someone and put it as cautiously as I can. And other times . . . Sorry, what was the question?

Interviewer: (question repeated)

Boy: It's straightforward in most respects because not a lot of people in my form know except, you know, the people that have been to my house and have seen. They've passed around the comment from form to form which gets me because if they were a friend, they wouldn't say things like that.

Interviewer: What kinds of things are said?

Boy: Well, I don't know. Eventually they find out and they guess for themselves, which I don't really mind. I shouldn't mind anyway. I get a bit annoyed at times because they do go on and they do make some rather nasty comments.

Girl: Problems with new people I meet. They want to know. Right now I'm in a school with my . . . two brothers . . . They all ask me why I'm darker than they are. It's hard to convince them that he is my brother until I go and talk to them.
Interviewer: So it's a bit awkward having to go through the explaining?
Girl: Yes. I dread it. I really dread it . . .

Boy: Not large ones (i.e., problems). Not ones I'd like to tell to my Mum and Dad because I don't think they'd probably understand because they are not brown or black.
Interviewer: Tell me a bit about the problems it gives you.
Boy: I get upset that it's just my colour that makes me inferior to someone else.
Interviewer: In what way?
Boy: I don't know what way they mean I'm inferior. It's just that they think I am and they call me Paki and all that.
Interviewer: Does that happen a lot?
Boy: Well, they sort of jokingly tease me and I said before they call me 'wog'. That doesn't upset me too much except that it keeps on happening and that I'm not one of them as a group sort of thing . . .

The majority of responses were coded as 'no problems'. The following are examples of some of the children who gave relatively full answers and yet were coded as 'no problems'.

Girl: Doesn't really give me any problems. Sometimes I quite like it because everybody else has to sunbathe madly and I already have it. I don't think it feels much different to if I was white.

And:

Girl: All straightforward . . . When I'm in the playground in the new school or something like that they say 'Why's your brother white?'
Interviewer: That happens quite a bit, has it?
Girl: Yes. It happened for about three weeks before everybody knew . . . They said, 'How come your brother's white?' . . . I used to say, 'Because he is' . . . or I just said I wasn't going to go into all that, so I just said, 'I'm adopted'. They hadn't got the faintest idea what that was so they just walked away.

Again, in the interests of accuracy, it is necessary to note that some of the children coded as 'no problems' did refer to what they seemed to consider as fairly minor problems or issues. Two responses can be used to illustrate this:

Girl: Don't give me any problems. And. I just. It's really just the same. I mean my family don't say anything about it and I don't think they're really bothered and I don't think they think, oh, you know . . . (child's name). They just treat me as anyone else, white, black or yellow.
Interviewer: Is it something you think about at all?

Girl: Yes. I do think about it. Sometimes I think that I wish I was white and sometimes I really wish I was darker. I think it's a shame that around here — there's not more darker people, which I really wish there was. I mean it's not that I don't like white people or anything like that. I can't say that, I mean I get on with them, but it's nice to have black people around because I prefer darker skin.* I mean, I don't know why, but I do. And I mean people at school . . . say things to me and that doesn't really bother me.

Interviewer: What sort of things do they say?

Girl: You know. Racialist things. But my friends stick up for me. Saying, 'You don't know what black is' and everything like that. But there's people much darker than me.

Interviewer: At school?

Girl: Yes. I mean, in our whole school there's only about seven people who are dark.

Interviewer: Out of how many?

Girl: Oh, about a thousand.

Boy: It's more or less straightforward really because I don't usually tell people I was adopted if I can help it.

Interviewer: Do they ask . . .?

Boy: No, they don't. Nobody usually asks because they don't really know. It doesn't really create very many problems. It's a bit odd sometimes walking along on the street and that sort of thing.

Interviewer: What, people looking at you?

Boy: It sometimes happens in shops, actually. They sometimes say, 'Are you together?' and we have to say yes . . . I don't really think about it very often, because most of the people around me — I don't see myself all the time so I don't really notice. None of my friends really react much.

Finally, the following response, although not representative, is a good example of the way in which children such as these may occasionally have to grapple with the meanings of the social world in which they find themselves:

Girl: Like when I'm looking to you, like I can see your face and you're white, but when, I can't see my face . . . So it doesn't. Like I know I'm brown, but I don't think about that. But probably, with a dog. She knows that she's a dog, but she thinks she's one of us. That's what I sort of mean.

Interviewer: Yes. I see what you mean. So what way does it give you problems?

Girl: Does it give me problems?

Interviewer: Perhaps that doesn't give you problems.

Girl: No.

Interviewer: Pretty straightforward?

Girl: Yes — straightforward.

---

* As the girl said this she was laughing. This illustrates the real problems of interpretation when sometimes the words alone are not sufficient to indicate the content of the response.

The responses to this question about how it 'feels' to be black in a white family again give little support to the notion that children adopted trans-racially will generally experience their position as problematic and conflicting. If such were the case, presumably we should have had a majority of the children talking about being 'upset', 'unhappy', 'out of it', 'not accepted' and 'loners'. Instead, the responses indicate that the majority define their position as not causing problems. Moreover, those that were coded as having 'problems' tended to talk about specific incidents and events (almost always outside the family) rather than describing *general* feelings.

Outside help

Concluding our investigation into difficulties the child might have experienced, we asked the parents whether the study child had 'ever had professional help for a personal or social problem'. Twenty-nine of the children had not had any such help. Of the remaining seven, two had had help from a speech therapist, one had had help from an educational psychologist and one from a social worker, one child had been involved in family therapy sessions and one had had help from one of the adoption workers in the original project. Finally, one child had had help from a number of sources, including an adoption worker, a social worker, child guidance, psychiatrist and a local GP.

Because of the possibility that adoptions may have an impact elsewhere in the family we asked a similar question about other children in the family. One child was an only child and out of the remaining 35 families, nine had had outside professional help for one or more of the siblings of the study child, ranging from speech therapy to family therapy. We also asked the nine parents whether they considered that the problems of these other children were related to having adopted the study child. Only one of the nine thought that this was the case.

Summary

In the previous chapter we examined the children's self-conceptions in terms of their racial background. We showed that there was little evidence to suggest that the children were developing positive perspectives on their racial origins and developing a sense of racial identity. In this chapter, we have taken the analysis a stage further to see if such self-perceptions are related to a lack of self-esteem and perceptions of the confusing and problematic nature of their lives.

Of course, much of the evidence we have presented earlier in this study is related to the issue of identity. Erikson, in his classic statement on 'identity diffusion' (a term he regarded as preferable to identity confusion), argued that such diffusion was likely to be evidenced by: (i) *a failure of intimacy* (the individual fears commitment or involvement in close interpersonal relationships); (ii) *diffusion of time perspective* (the individual finds it impossible to plan for the future or to retain any sense of time); (iii) *diffusion of industry* (the individual finds it difficult to harness his or her resources in a realistic way in work or study) and (iv) *negative identity* (the individual selects an identity exactly opposite to that preferred by parents and other important adults).[9] If these are the primary indicators, then the evidence presented earlier in this study on the children's life inside and outside the family does not support a conclusion of identity diffusion.

Such a conclusion is not supported either by the specific data presented in this chapter. One of the crucial constituents of a confused identity is a devalued sense of self-esteem: not knowing who she is, the child has a low opinion of her own value. The results of the two self-esteem tests described in this chapter show no signs of this.

Also, if the children are experiencing their lives and family settings as very difficult, we could expect that this might be illustrated by some level of behaviour disorder. The results of the Rutter scales completed by parents and teachers show no evidence of this in all but a very few cases.

These test results were consistent with our own interview responses. In the answers to the question about how it 'feels' to be black in a white family there was little evidence of anxiety, conflict, uncertainty and the children grappling with confusion related to origins. Some of the children did refer to difficulties and problems, but these were related to specific situations and individuals. We would not wish to minimise these problems and difficulties because, as some of the responses in this chapter indicate, they are experienced as far from pleasant. But in terms of identity one of the crucial factors seems to be that the children are able to contain these events in particular areas of their lives. They do not come to control the child's *general* conception of herself. On our evidence we must conclude that the significance attached to identity confusion in transracially adopted children is based either on the investigations of a small number of such children who have presented for therapy, or on the assumption that such identity confusion is what *ought* to happen.

9

Experiencing being 'coloured'

A further criticism of transracial adoption (see Chapter 1) is that, as the child is not brought up in a black family, she has none of the survival skills necessary for 'coping' in a white society; racial background becomes highly significant for the child and is experienced as problematic.

American research has shown how the black family operates to give the child such skills.[1] Writers on transracial adoption, both in the United States and this country, have echoed this theme. For instance, Chestang has written that

> The black child reared in his own community can at least retreat to his own people for solace when the situation demands it. What of the black child who is defined as an alien in the white community and a traitor in the black community? Obviously such a child would be under inordinate stress and he would be likely to crumble under tension.[2]

More recently and nearer to home, Mary James has argued that

> there are certain social survival techniques that white parents just cannot teach their black children and experiences that they cannot share. Their child will need to look to other black adults or black friends in order to learn these skills. This is not possible for a child cut off from his own community.[3]

As in earlier chapters, therefore, we are again in the position of having to compare these criticisms with the reported experiences and feelings of the BAP children. If the arguments against transracial adoption are to be supported, the children would have to report that racial background is of considerable and problematic significance in their lives and that they are unable to 'cope' with being black in a white family.

In this chapter, therefore, we describe our attempts to get at something of the everyday character of the children's lives, to examine the place of racial background in those lives and also to explore how racial background is dealt with and 'managed' by the children.

The significance of racial background in the children's lives

Following Kitwood[4] we asked the study children to describe events in their

91

lives which corresponded to general situations described to them. The question asked is presented here in full to demonstrate the approach that we used:

> People go through ups and downs in their lives and a lot of different things happen to them. They also have a lot of different feelings about things. I want you to think about your own life and try and describe different things happening to you and how you felt about them. So, for instance, if I say 'a time when I felt happy', you might say when you did well at school on a particular occasion, or you might describe an especially good birthday you had.
> A time I was really happy.
> A time I was really unhappy.
> A time I was proud of myself.
> A time I was ashamed of myself.
> A time I felt I had a lot of friends.
> A time I felt all alone.
> A time I wished I could have discussed a problem with a helpful adult, but couldn't find one.

This approach proved successful in that the children were able to comprehend its purpose and also, as it was dealing with concrete experiences, to give full replies. We believe the responses give a good idea of the character of the lives that the children were leading and what they regarded as significant.

There was a great variety in the answers, but it was possible to analyse them to give us clues about the significance to the children of their racial background. If the children regarded their racial background as being overwhelmingly or significantly problematic, then it seems reasonable to expect that this would show up in answers to, for instance, 'a time I was really unhappy', 'a time I felt all alone'. We are as confident as we can be that this line of questioning was one of the most appropriate ways of getting at their feelings about their lives and the significance of racial background in their everyday experience.

In answering this question only six of the 36 children made any reference to their racial background; four were boys and two were mixed-race. Without reproducing the transcripts of all the replies it is impossible fully to show the variety of experiences, events and feelings that were referred to. But to give an idea of the nature of the replies that this question produced the full transcript from one interview is given below. This response was coded as 'racial background not referred to'.

Interviewer: A time I was really happy.

Girl: Um — At this school disco I went to and we were just really having fun. I really enjoyed that.

Interviewer: Why?

Girl: Because everybody's nicer to each other out of school, I think. Forget the bitchiness and everything and, just prancing about. (Laughs) It sounds stupid, but having a nice time —

Interviewer: Right. A time I was really unhappy.

Girl: Uh — When my French teacher last year, she — I don't know — we just didn't get on. But this year we get on really well. And she phoned up my Mum and started complaining about me and when I came home Mum had a go at me. I really hated it then.

Interviewer: Was it unfair?

Girl: Um — Yes, I, I think it was because everybody said, 'Gosh, she really picks on you'. But now she doesn't this year, and I've been doing better work for her and everything. It's cleared itself up. It was a bit stupid, really — I used to get in a mood with her and she used to get in a mood with me.

Interviewer: You didn't work?

Girl: No. (laughs)

Interviewer: Right. Now the next one. A time I was proud of myself.

Girl: Oh. When I first started my music lessons and I did Grade I and I got 141 out of 50 (laughs) — I mean out of 150 — and that was the best mark. Everybody said, 'Oh, that's the best mark I've ever heard of', and . . . was pleased with me and Mum was pleased with me and so were Dad and my music teacher . . .

Interviewer: Well. A time I was ashamed of myself.

Girl: Um (laughs) Oh, I bet . . . Oh, I know, when I got 21 per cent in a Maths test. I felt awful. I was in the top Maths set as well (laughs) That was awful because he read everybody's mark out, and he started from the top and said so-and-so has got 90 per cent, and I thought, oh, that's good, expecting myself to be read out soon. It went lower and lower — well, quite a few people were grouped at the bottom about around 30s, and I got the very lowest — well, in my class, but not in the whole year because some people were much worse than me, about 2 per cent. That was pretty awful. (laughs)

Interviewer: Oh dear. A time I felt I had a lot of friends.

Girl: Oh, one day I said I was going to the cinema with Jane and she was due to come back and spend the night. And then Anne phoned me up . . . and asked me to go somewhere, I can't remember. And then, later, Jean and Bella came round and asked me to go to . . . with them . . . (laughs) I thought, 'Oh!' It was quite annoying. Sometimes I sit there wishing somebody would ring me and then it all happens at once. I ended up with Jane. She was the first one.

Interviewer: Now, a time I felt all alone.

Girl: Um — oh, ages ago, at Middle School. I used to go round with this girl, these two girls, called Tracey and Frances and — I can't remember what the argument was about — and they went off for about a month. And I'd stuck with them for ages and hadn't really circulated with anybody else. So for the first week of that month I hardly spoke to anybody, or anything. I was really annoyed with them for leaving me. But after that I made friends with some other people there. It's all worked out OK.

Interviewer: Right. Now the last one. A time I wished I could have discussed a problem with a helpful adult, but couldn't find one.

Girl: Mm — can't really think. I just can't really think of one.

Six children referred to their racial background in responding to this question, but even for these it could not be said that racial background was a dominant ingredient of the replies. The following full response of one of these six indicates the balance:

Interviewer: A time I was really happy. Can you think of a time that fits that?

Boy: Well, it must have been, it was about five years ago, I think. We used to go down . . . in the sea front and this playground, this kind of fair, sort of thing and the seaside and that. And I used to like that.

Interviewer: Did you go quite regularly?

Boy: No. We just do about once a year. That's what made it sort of, looking forward to it.

Interviewer: Right. A time I was really unhappy.

Boy: Really unhappy.

Interviewer: Yes. It could be sort of moderately unhappy if you can't think of the terribly unhappy one.

Boy: Well, sort of, you know, a bit of stick at school because of my colour, like, you know. Sometimes I get a bit down about it, but

Interviewer: What, from the other kids?

Boy: Yeah. Not, not people I know and that. It's usually sort of . . . about three years older than me, you know.

Interviewer: Is it a big school where you can't sort of know everybody?

Boy: Know everyone in my year now, but . . . school.

Interviewer: A time I was proud of myself.

Boy: At junior school we did a bit of art work. Sort of a great big poster, sort of . . . I think. And they did a great big picture of it up on the, in the assembly hall, I think. That was about a year ago.

Interviewer: A time I was ashamed of myself.

Boy: Sometimes I feel like doing down myself. I know it's likely to sort of get a bit of stick, so I just don't think about it or, of course, I'm a fatty or something like that. Then afterwards I think that I shouldn't have done that. Somehow I don't feel. So I don't do it any more or . . .

Interviewer: A time I thought I had a lot of friends.

Boy: Mm, parties and things like that, you know.

Interviewer: A time I felt all alone.

Boy: Well, once when I was little, I seem to remember getting lost in a big store or

something like that. I think I started crying. But I can't remember anything sort
of . . .

Interviewer: A time I wished I could have discussed a problem with a helpful adult,
but couldn't find one.

Boy: No. I can't.

Interviewer: No? All right.

This, then, is an example of the six children who made reference to their
racial background in their answers. From the responses to this question it
would, of course, be naive to conclude that racial background was significant
for only six of the children. Such a reduction of qualitative material to quan-
titative conclusions does injustice to the nature and complexity of the
children's lives and the variety of responses that the question produced.
Nevertheless, from this question we can find no evidence of the overriding
significance of racial background in terms of how these children experience
their lives. What we obtain from the answers is a picture of the interests, feelings and experience of a group of primarily middle-class children as they
enter and go through adolescence.

Also of interest is that only seven of the 36 could describe situations in
answer to the question 'a time I wished I could have discussed a problem
with a helpful adult, but couldn't find one'. Three of these seven were also in
the group of six who were coded as 'racial background referred to'. This tells
us something about the isolation or lack of it that the children experienced
and also perhaps the help of caring people inside and outside the family to
whom they had access.

Experiencing colour

The study children were also asked to describe 'a time I was proud to be
coloured/black/brown', 'a time I wished I was white', 'a time I felt I had a lot
of friends because I was coloured/black/brown', and 'a time I felt alone
because I was coloured/black/brown'. Again, the approach was effective in
that the children could understand its purpose and most were able to give
full answers. Some were unable to give us experiences that were relevant,
but this represents data in its own right. One boy rather sadly said when we
asked him to describe a time when he was proud to be Indian, 'That's not
cropped up yet'.

Also, the question produced some responses that went beyond the
straightforward reporting of events. Here, for instance, is one of the boys'
answer to the 'proud' question:

Um, I don't look, I don't look upon myself as being coloured, if you see what I mean, because although — I can't explain it because I, I know, I know people that are dark-skinned, but they're with their proper family, but, so people, a lot of people don't notice with me. And in the summer a lot of people just think I'm sunburnt.

This and other such replies convinced us of the appropriateness of this line of questioning for entering into the experience of these children.

Being proud

Sixteen of the 36 children could describe situations in which they had been 'proud to be coloured/black/brown'. Of these, eight gave experiences relating to not having to go into the sun to get a suntan. For example:

Girl: I don't, um, I think, um, being my colour — not exactly brown — I think it makes me proud nearly every summer when I get this lovely tan. You know, I think 'lucky me'. I mean everybody's saying, 'Coo, aren't you lucky!' I don't get a very deep tan, but some people who don't, you know, who just stay white, quite white, and who have to sunbathe for it, you know, I get quite proud then.

Boy: It was basically a joke because I was laughing at all these people that were going out to the Boots and everything and having to buy suntan lotion, I mean, I was laughing my head off. If you can get to the stage I am, say, within a week, I'll give you a . . ., you know.

Two indicated they were 'proud all the time', and of the remaining six, one said she was proud 'when we talk about Martin Luther King', and another because he was not affected by the heat. Two responses seemed to indicate that, although of a different racial background, the children were being accepted or doing just as well as their white contemporaries:

Girl: A time I was — oh, it's hard. Um, lately I've been, very recently I've been proud when — Maybe it's because my friends, um, sort of say, 'Oh, I count you as white' and everything like that, and I'd prefer not to be. So I've got more proud of it, if that makes sense. But I can't sort of say, oh, when

Girl: With school work, um, when I did well in exams and I felt because I was coloured I could do better and just as well as other people.

One gave a response indicating that he could move with ease between two social worlds and visit his black friends at home, and, finally, one boy replied in distinctly pragmatic terms, saying that he was very ambitious at football and if there were any scouts from the big clubs watching, he would stand out.

Wishing to be white

Nineteen of the 36 children could tell us about situations in which they had wished they were white. Of these, nine referred to situations of being made fun of or teasing from their contemporaries:

Girl: When I get called names.

Boy: Oh, lots of them keeps laughing at me sometimes, things like that. Not really.

Boy: Um, when, um, when the, um, well, the other children used to tease me when I was about eleven, I think. I thought, 'Oh, I wish I was white' and I think that's the only time.

Two referred to school, although it was not clear whether this was in relation to general difficulties or difficulties specifically with peers. One of these answered 'juniors' and the other answered:

Boy: When I was the only brown person in the class, and all the others were white.

Of the remaining eight children, three said that it was 'all the time'. One boy told us it was 'when the skinheads come along' and a girl told us that it was when she went to the local club where there were National Front sympathisers.

One child told us that it was at school concerts and festivals when white children always seemed to do best, and one told us that she felt envious of white hairstyles:

Girl: Um — well, sometimes I'd like to have straight hair because it annoys me, being curly hair and never being able to do anything with it. When somebody comes with a really nice hairstyle that I'd like to have. I'd like to have straight hair, but I wouldn't really want to be white because I like being brown because I think tans look nice (laughs)

Finally, one girl who was attending boarding school gave a nice example of the lack of understanding which these children sometimes have to face:

Girl: Oh, one time, it was just recently, really, and they had these teachers on night duty — they go round and turn the lights off — and she was talking to us, I don't know how it came about, but, you know, it came on to religion — we were probably talking about RE — and she asked me one of these things about Hindus' religion. I got a bit fed up with that. She didn't really understand, so I got fed up with that.

A lot of friends

Only three of the children could describe a time when they felt they had 'a lot

97

of friends' because of being coloured/black/brown. One, after describing how another had 'called her names' because of her colour, told us:

> *Girl:* Well, they would tell me to ignore her and somebody called her names, but I don't know what. But it got really bad after a while — not fighting or anything — but another teacher came in to see about it, and they all stuck up for me there, they all said how she had been calling me names.

Another girl, who was one of the four children who were living in something approaching a multi-racial area, told us:

> *Girl:* When I was, um, cops came up to us and started leaning 'cos I was coloured.
> *Interviewer:* Tell me about that.
> *Girl:* Oh, I was just standing there waiting for somebody and he said, 'Who are you waiting for?' And I said 'I'm waiting for some friends' and he said, 'I hope you're not going to cause trouble' and he was sort of very . . . you know, because he likes doing that — he's sort of well known for doing it. And they came up and if I hadn't been coloured, they wouldn't have said anything, you know.
> *Interviewer:* This was friends of yours?
> *Girl:* Well, yes. I mean some of them won't even . . ., but half of them were my friends, and because I was sort of mixed in any coloured they did come and sort of say, no, sort of, lay off. The coppers are crafty and if you lay a finger on them, if you hit them for insulting you, then, they'll get you done for assaulting a copper, you know? It's wicked.

All alone

Of the 36 children, nine could recount for us situations in which they had 'felt alone because I was coloured/black/brown'. Two of these described starting at a new school and feeling alone. One of them said:

> *Boy:* When you first go to school or something like that.
> *Interviewer:* Does it make it harder, d'you reckon, to make friends?
> *Boy:* At first. Yes, I should think so.
> *Interviewer:* How long d'you think that goes on for?
> *Boy:* Not that long. Sort of . . . two months, I should think — something like that.

Two of the nine talked about school when they were younger. One told us:

> *Girl:* Yes, well, it's school, my old school. I mean sometimes, mainly when I was younger. But I suppose as you get older you get closer to your friends, don't you? I mean, when I was younger, I don't really remember.

Two of them described specific situations at school which involved the content of lessons. One described a discussion in social studies about whether 'blacks are equal' in which she 'couldn't really say anything' and a boy told us:

> *Boy:* A time in class when, say, geography or something, and he sort of starts talking about coloured people and that. Feel a bit embarrassed sometimes — sort of picking me out. Thinking that I know everything about the country.

Two of the nine talked specifically about peer-group relations, one commenting:

> *Boy:* When all, when all the whites, they all went off to do something and I didn't go, and, you know, I felt
> *Interviewer:* Why was that? Why didn't you go?
> *Boy:* Because I sort of, I didn't sort of fit in, I just . . . sort of thing.

Finally, one boy talked about feeling alone because of colour when he moved from London to an almost entirely white area.

The answers to 'times when' questions give us clues on the relative frequency of these different experiences in the children's lives. More of the children could describe situations in which they wished they were white than in which they were 'proud to be black/brown/coloured', although about half could describe events in the latter category. Equally important, the responses to this question give us insights into the nature of the children's experience of their colour. We begin to get a picture of the place of racial background in the lives of these children and the variety of experiences which such children may encounter.

Experiencing aggression

Besides attempting to assess the general significance of racial background in the children's lives, we also asked a more direct question: 'Looking back can you remember people being nasty or unpleasant about your different racial background? I'm particularly interested in what they have said or done to be unpleasant'. The interviewer instructions on this question were to attempt to get at what actually happened, at what age it occurred, how they coped with it, what they thought of the people involved, whether they told their parents and how they reacted, and whether it was 'serious' or 'mickey-taking'.

As this question came relatively late on in the interview schedule some of the children had already referred to situations in which people were 'nasty or unpleasant' about their different racial background and several of these have been included in the analysis of the responses to this question.

The question was not an easy one to ask because it was attempting to get at

99

situations which by their nature would have perhaps been experienced as distressing by the children. Because of this, interviewers used their judgement to omit all or part of the question where this seemed appropriate.

There is also a difficulty, as with all such retrospective questioning, that the events are described with present-day interpretations. And, finally, there is a difficulty in assessing when exactly the events described occurred. Particularly when the events described occurred at Junior School the children were vague about their ages, saying such things as, 'perhaps when I was seven or eight'.

However, despite certain limitations of the data, we are able to analyse it in a number of ways. Only six (of 35 who were asked) said that they could not remember people being 'nasty or unpleasant' about their different racial background. One of these made the distinction between people being nasty or unpleasant and 'jokes':

> *Girl:* Well, some people just joke. You know, they say, 'Oh, hullo Michael Jackson' and things like that. I don't really mind because I think it's quite funny and everybody gets called a few names. I'd have to say it's jokes — I don't think it's anything else. That's all really.
>
> *Interviewer:* Is it just jokes? Has anybody actually been nasty to you? Somebody tried to be hurtful?
>
> *Girl:* No.

The remaining 29 children could remember such events, and all referred to people of their own age being 'nasty or unpleasant'. None of the situations described involved adults.

For three children, it was impossible to identify precisely when the described events had occurred. Eighteen described events which had occurred at least a year before and in the majority of cases at least two or three years previously. Most were either during their first years at school or on their move to their secondary school. Here, for instance, are two children talking about their early years at school:

> *Girl:* Yes, I can remember it. I can remember at Primary School I used to come home and cry and my Mum — you see, I used to bottle it up and then I just started crying one day and Mum told me to wait till I came home and tell her . . . At Primary School I was the only darker one there. So of course they had to say something, but I think — well, I mean everyone says something, it's just — I think it was more to me than — I mean, everyone's horrible to everyone else, but I think it was more to me. But that's not really surprising because I *was* different — am different. But . . . the difference isn't so noticeable now, really. Not so — I don't know — not so important, but it's something to say, isn't it, and so they said (it).

And:

> *Girl:* Uh. I remember once in the Juniors, like . . . arguing, things like that, and they said, um, something like, 'Go back to your own country' and things like that. But I suppose they was young then and it doesn't really bother me now. Though it did bother me *then*.

Others experienced unpleasantness when they started secondary school:

> *Girl:* Yeah, I remember a boy in the First Year, when I was in the First Year . . . He started calling me names or started calling me things, so I grabbed him by the hair and made him apologise.
> *Interviewer:* Did he ever do it again?
> *Girl:* No.
> *Interviewer:* So one way of dealing with him. Was that the only time that that happened?
> *Girl:* Uh, no. I've been teased at Primary School, didn't take too much notice, though.

And:

> *Girl:* That was at the beginning of Primary School, and then nobody did until I came down to the Comprehensive because there were lots of people, you know, I mean, it's right up to the Sixth Form and I don't, I didn't really know that many people apart from the people who came with me.

Eight children talked about more recent peer-group incidents. For instance:

> *Girl:* Well, I trusted this girl. Well, she knew that I was a different colour to the family. She wanted to know so I told her that I was adopted and she was really surprised, you know. Then next — oh, I don't know — we had an argument one day and she passed it round the whole class and, you know, I just stood there and they was making fun of me, you know, the colour really and they were passing it round that I was adopted, and that's it.

What does seem to be evident from the interviews is that not all of the children appeared to be 'upset' by the incidents. One of the ones who did report being 'upset' told us:

> *Boy:* I can, yes. Some, well boys are, when I — it doesn't really bother me now, but in the Middle School when I was, say, eleven, it really did use to bother me and I think I done the wrong thing in trying to get back at them, and I think that's silly because I should have just left them and let them get on with it . . . And I think I done the wrong thing by trying to go against them and if I, you know, just left them alone, I think they'd have been, after a while, I think they would have taken to me and I think I would have had more friends.

101

We suspect, however, that some of the children were more upset by these incidents than they were prepared to admit, either to themselves or to the interviewer. In addition, the passage of time may have made some of the incidents seem less distressing than at the time. Also, the children talked in terms which indicated that they had had to develop their own 'coping mechanisms'. For instance, one child told us it was 'just teasing' and that he treated it 'as a great joke' and said, 'it depends how sensitive you are'. Another coped with the experience by saying it was only a 'silly' minority, and a third told us that it did happen, but only very infrequently:

Boy: No. I haven't really noticed anybody in particular that stands out from anybody else. It's not as if someone noticed it every day and it happens every day; it just happens very occasionally and it hasn't happened at all recently.
Interviewer: What, sort of like an odd comment or something?
Boy: Mm, and just a thing that you wouldn't take any notice of.

Some children took a more aggressive stance:

Girl: No. I think I'd make fun of people who normally do that. I pretend I can't speak English. Um, I really gee them up, you know, because I thought if they've got the cheek to say that, I don't see why I can't piss about either. Everyone's . . . to their opinion, I suppose. I just don't like people classing one group of people as something like that.

And, as was indicated by another response, reactions need not be only verbal:

Girl: Yes. It was only a . . . it was only small. And it was raining and we had to stay inside and he kept mocking me about it.
Interviewer: What kind of things was he saying?
Girl: He was calling me names.
Interviewer: I see. How did you deal with that? What happened? Did you tell the teacher, did you tell Mum and Dad, or what?
Girl: (Laughs) It was much more than that. He had to have . . . stitches in it.
Interviewer: He had what?
Girl: Them paper-fly stitches in his nose.
Interviewer: He had, how many stitches did he have?
Girl: I don't know. He had just black and white . . . on his nose.

Finally, in our analysis of responses about people being 'nasty or unpleasant', it is worth noting a point made by at least two children in answer to this question. They described for us how once they had become established in their social groups, then the difficulties ceased. This would be consistent with the responses of those children who said such incidents were experienced when they started at their new school. One girl explained this in the following way:

Girl: Well, just called me nig-nog and things like that, but I didn't really take any notice.

Interviewer: Were they trying to be nasty, or was it just nasty anyway even though they didn't mean to be?

Girl: Well, people usually say it to cause attention, but I didn't, you know. But no one calls it me now, you know, 'cos I'm just one of, I'm a person, just a person from . . . School, so nobody says anything.

The evidence from these reported memories suggests that problematic events and incidents were experienced when the children were establishing themselves in their social groups and that by the time they had reached adolescence they were living in social worlds in which they were relatively well-established and saw their racial background as creating fewer problems.

Summary

This chapter has presented some of the children's experiences of being of a different racial background to the people around them. This provides not only information about the kinds of events likely to be experienced by such children, but further evidence with which to evaluate transracial adoption.

There are, of course, dangers in trying to combine the stories or 'biographies' of these children to produce a composite picture. The children are individuals leading individual lives in sometimes quite dissimilar social and physical surroundings. Yet there does seem a consistency in many of the responses and, as interviewers, we were struck by the similarities in the ways in which many of the children described, experienced and reacted to their racial background.

The majority of children had certainly experienced some difficulties related to racial background. More than half could describe situations in which they 'wished they had been white' and more had experienced situations of being alone than had experienced situations of having a lot of friends because of racial background. On the other hand, half of the children could describe situations of having been 'proud' to be black/brown/coloured. Others made no reference to racial background at all.

Combining the various strands of evidence presented in this chapter, it seems that although racial background did cause its difficulties, and in general was experienced as having more disadvantages than advantages, the children did not consider these to be of overriding significance in their lives. And, when faced with situations in which racial background was problematic, the large majority were able effectively to deal with them so that they did not impinge too dangerously on their sense of self-worth. Despite the white family setting they had learned their 'techniques of coping'.

Critics of transracial adoption have argued that it is at adolescence that the experience of colour will become increasingly problematic. Evidence from this study suggests that the majority of children saw the difficulties as having occurred considerably earlier in their lives. And, as we saw in Chapter 6, this view is consistent with that of the parents.

10

Being adopted

The previous four chapters have concentrated on racial differences and what effect these are perceived as having in the family and the outside world. It is difficult to isolate the issues involved, but in terms of how the children see themselves, the fact of being adopted may be of more significance than being of a different racial background. Also, of course, being a different colour from the parents highlights the fact of adoption. While children adopted by parents of the same racial background can choose to whom and when they disclose their adoptive status, these youngsters and their parents may be required to give explanations all through their lives. They could be seen as a family perpetually 'in the making'. New situations, such as new schools, holidays and moves of house, may arouse curiosity and speculation as to how the family came about and, indeed, how permanent the arrangement is.

Added to this, it has been recognised that adolescence perhaps has difficulties for all adopted children. For instance, Sarosky has noted that

> when the adoptee reaches adolescence he/she has a special interest in the nature of his/her conception, the reason for the adoption and his/her genealogical history. Unfortunately, this healthy curiosity is often construed by the adoptive parents as an indication that they failed in their role as parents or a sign of their child's lack of love for them.[1]

In this chapter, therefore, we concentrate on the issues surrounding adoption and how the parents and children have 'dealt' with the fact of being adopted.

Contact with other adoptive families

If the adoptive families are in touch with other such families, on either a formal or informal basis, then this provides a forum for discussing adoption-related issues if necessary. It also gives their children a chance to have contact with families that have been created in the same way as their own.

We asked the parents, 'Do you belong to any organisation or support groups related to adoption?' Only two of the 36 couples said they had links with an adoptive parents' group and even in those two cases the contact was limited. The remaining parents did not belong to such groups.

We then asked the parents, 'Do you have any friends who have adopted black or Asian children?' Twenty-five couples said they did not; six said they knew one other couple, four said they knew three and one couple said they knew more than three.

Five of the 25 families that did not have friends who had adopted black or Asian children were in the group of eight who had adopted younger black children. But this still leaves 20 of the children who did not know any others who were in a similar situation.

Talking about adoption

We asked the parents, 'What is your approach to discussing his/her first parents and why he/she was adopted? Do you start conversations about it or do you wait until he/she asks?' We coded the parents of five children as having a policy of 'initiating conversations', the parents of seven as having no clearly defined policy and the parents of 18 as 'waiting until the child asks'. In addition to this, the parents of four children were coded as 'impossible to answer: topic comes up very rarely'; one response was impossible to code and one couple appeared to operate two policies, the mother sometimes initiating conversations and the father waiting until the topic came up.

The following are examples of the parents whom we coded as initiating conversations:

> *Father:* I've tried to dig it up once or twice deliberately, but there's been no interest so it's just disappeared.
> *Interviewer:* Does she ever ask?
> *Father:* No. Not a lot, no.

And:

> *Father:* Well, I don't think she would ever ask.
> *Mother:* She wouldn't ask anything directly. It would be something like, 'What time of day was I born?' And then you'd pick up from that. I would never deal with it in isolation, it would just arise out of something. You make the opening and then if she didn't take it up, I think I would ignore it. I'd let it drop.

The following are examples of the seven families in which there seemed to be no clearly-defined policy:

> *Father:* It comes up with such reasonable frequency that there's no need to initiate it.
> *Mother:* I usually expand on it a bit. I tend to seize the moment and go on a bit.

106

Father: . . . rather than dismiss it.
. . . It tends to happen at mealtimes when we're all involved.

And:

Mother: It's something that comes up. We wouldn't start to talk about India or . . . or adoption. I think, really, you're too busy just getting along and living.
Father: They both think that they were chosen by us.
Mother: Yes, that often comes up.

Most people waited for the children to initiate the topic. Some parents had previously tried to start conversations, but no longer did this and waited for the children to ask:

Mother: I wouldn't dare to start a conversation on the topic now! (laughter) She'd say, 'Oh, Mum, not all about that again now!'
Father: We did at one stage.
Interviewer: Your original policy was to initiate conversations?
Mother: Yes. And we did work through all that.
Father: Just to give her the opportunity to see if she responded.
Mother: And she did at one time. I remember having long conversations about it, but not any more.
Father: She worked it through. Got it straight.

And:

Father: Apart from filling in the facts that she was adopted, we've always done that, but we've, for further information, we've waited for her to ask.
Mother: Occasionally she asks one or two questions coming out of a TV programme or something like that. She takes it from there — she relates it to herself and then she comes out with a little question. Otherwise she never — she's not an inquisitive sort of child. She's pretty settled and I don't think it would worry her if she didn't know anything.

Others seemed anxious not to upset the equilibrium of the relationship. They felt that by waiting for the child to ask the questions, fewer upsets would occur.

Father: I always wait. I would never bring it up, it might upset her.
Mother: I think it's something that must come from her. It's got to be her interest. I think, well, why should she think it bothers me to bring it up.

And:

Father: We would certainly never start such a conversation. I don't see any point in it. As far as she's concerned I'm pretty sure that it's either deeply buried or she genuinely has no curiosity. And I'm not sure which. But, either way, it would be perhaps a dangerous thing for us to do to start her out on it . . . It is very occasionally touched on in the course of some general family conversation.

Others felt that it could be of more interest to the child in the future in the natural course of events, but that it is best for the child to set the pace:

> *Father:* I would anticipate it coming up in the next couple of years — I've no basis for saying that, but you read of people who've been adopted trying to find out about their parents.
> *Mother:* She has asked once about doing that.
> *Father:* On the other hand, because she's apparently had unrestricted access to all the information that we have, it may not be so pressing for her. But I wouldn't be surprised if in the next couple of years she wanted to find out more.

Finally, the following is an example of one of those families in which the topic arose so rarely that it was impossible to answer:

> *Mother:* No, it's not something we talk about. I don't think any of us feel adoption is very special or different. We always talked about it. I used to tell him the story before he was old enough to hold a conversation . . . I think that's why he's never asked too many questions.

The children were also asked, 'If you want to talk about your first parents or your adoption, do you start the conversation or do you wait until your parents start the conversation?' Twenty-one of the children said that they would 'start the conversation', three said they would wait for their parents to start and one said she couldn't talk to her parents about it. In the remaining 11 cases it was either impossible to code or, more usually, the children indicated that it came up so infrequently that it was impossible to answer.

The following are representative answers from the 21 children who said they would 'start the conversation':

> *Girl:* Oh, I'd start the conversation. I'd just ask with no dismay.
> *Interviewer:* Why's that? Because you always start it or
> *Girl:* Well. Well, they talk to me about it and it's not sort of hushed up or anything. So if I wanted to know something, I'd just ask them.

And:

> *Girl:* I think they know that I'd come to them.
> *Interviewer:* They know that you'd come to them?
> *Girl:* Because, I mean, they've told me that I was adopted, you know, and of course I know anyway, but they, they'd probably wait until I had a problem or something because they wouldn't be able to know exactly when and that.

108

Several children indicated that, although they would introduce the subject if and when they wanted to discuss something about their adoption, the subject arose infrequently. One child, for instance, told us that the family did not 'avoid it', but that it did not usually crop up. And the following are examples of the children who said it came up so infrequently that they could not really say who introduced it:

Boy: It's on a rare occasion that Mum will bring up something about it.
Interviewer: I see. But she brings it up, rather than you, than you ask, usually, does she?
Boy: Mm, I don't know. It's a bit of both.
Interviewer: I see.
Boy: It's just the odd comment, you know. We don't go into long, detailed discussions. We don't, you know, we don't usually bring that up.

And:

Girl: Well, we don't talk about it.
Interviewer: You don't talk about it?
Girl: No, because, um, they chose me, as you know. My Mother says sometimes, 'Oh, I've had' (laughs) she sometimes thinks she's had me. She keeps on forgetting.
Interviewer: That's great. Tell me about that.
Girl: Sometimes we're in the car and she says, um, this actually happened, but I can't remember when it was, She said, oh, 'When I had you, you were' and she goes 'ooh!' (laughs). I don't feel any different. They're like my mum and dad. My real mum and dad.

In one case the child indicated that she would not start the conversation with her parents, but would raise it with someone outside the family at a later stage:

Girl: No, I wouldn't talk to them about things . . . When I'm older I'll probably sort of contact somebody in the adoption thing, that would know more about it really.
Interviewer: So you'd leave it like that. You wouldn't really talk to
Girl: No.

And, finally, the following is an example of the small group of children (four) who said they would wait for parents to start the conversation:

I wait for them to do it because, as far as I'm concerned, I've got to look to the future, not look back at the past.

We speculated beforehand that there might be families in which both parents and child were waiting for the other to initiate discussion about adoption, resulting in no discussion at all.[2] To examine this we were able to compare the responses of the children with those of the parents. In 27 of the families there appeared to be no such breakdown of communication in the sense that:

— the parents said they initiated conversations and the child said she did;
— parents and child agreed it was wholly or in part the job of the parent to initiate conversations, and
— parents and child agreed that it was wholly or in part the job of the child to initiate conversations.

These 27 families could be described as having a working relationship in which somebody in the home initiates discussion; each person was not apparently waiting for the other to begin. This is not to say that adoption was frequently discussed. In at least 20 of the families one member spontaneously commented how little the subject was discussed. For many families their response had a hypothetical ring to it, i.e., 'if he wanted to know, he would ask'.

One of the remaining nine cases was the family in which the child said she could not talk to her parents about being adopted. In the other eight families there was some evidence of a family system in which there was no consistency of perception about who should start conversations, leading to a possible situation in which it was not discussed at all. The most frequent potential inconsistency was the parents saying that they waited for the child to initiate conversations and the child saying it came up so infrequently that it was impossible to answer. In one case the parents stated that the subject came up so often in a natural way that they could not say who usually initiated it. In contrast, their child said:

> *Girl:* Oh, we don't really talk about it. You know. When I heard you were coming, I sort of asked a few questions. You know, I sort of, you know, I was just curious and I was sort of asking things about myself a bit, but, other than that, we don't really talk about it at all.
>
> *Interviewer:* Is that how you like it to be?
>
> *Girl:* Yes. I mean, I don't want it to be wiped out, but, on the other hand, I don't want it to be, you know, I'm just happy like this. You know. I don't want it to interfere. But I don't want to forget it, 'cos, you know, it wouldn't be right forgetting it, I don't think.

What the parents talk about

At the time of their adoption the adoptive parents were given written details of their child's background, including brief descriptions of the natural parents' appearance, education, occupation, personality and hobbies. In some cases, the details were more complete than others. The information was usually more thorough for the natural mother than for the natural father. These descriptions tended to be limited to brief details about the natural parents as individuals rather than to their reasons for relinquishing their child for adoption.

In the interviews the parents were asked, 'Can you tell me/remind me about what you have told him/her about his/her first parents and why he/she was adopted? Have you modified or expanded on this as he/she got older? If yes, in what ways?'

It was impossible to code responses to this question, but the following transcripts indicate the range of the information that had been given to the children. A small group of the parents were in a position to give, and had given, fairly full information:

Mother: When, as time's gone by, we've told him everything we know, haven't we? The first thing he knew was that we saw him in London and he came home in a big black car. We were given quite a lot of information about his parents. He knows that his first mother had been an art student and that both his grandmothers were teachers. He knows his father was training to be an accountant . . . I don't think we've said in so many words that they weren't married. But it's been assumed.

And:

Mother: It's a long while ago . . . What did I tell her? Well, it was in story form at that time. She's read all her letters now so she knows all there is to know. Her mother was a very nice person. That she wanted to keep her but circumstances wouldn't allow. We've not really mentioned anything about her father — he's always been a shadowy figure. She does know he was West Indian. But it's so long ago . . .

Interviewer: Have you expanded the story at all as she's grown up or are there any bits you've kept back?

Mother: Nothing has been said for almost years. She's read all her papers. When she was about ten she said could she read them all again. And she knows she could always see them again if she wanted to refresh her mind.

Father: If there was a programme on adoption, then we would mention it . . . I think I would tend to play it down. Wouldn't want her to think that she was any different from the others.

Many parents said they have given the child a considerable amount of information in the past, but met with a lack of response or interest on the part of their child:

Interviewer: In terms of what you have told her about her first mother and father, have you expanded on that or modified it? Or explained it in different ways?

Mother: I think probably we haven't much because she's shown such little interest . . . Not much. If ever an opportunity arises and I start to talk about it, she says, 'Oh, don't go on so'. She thinks I'm over-explaining and I think she knows why I'm over-explaining — because it's something I feel she ought to know about, but she kind of tells me off. 'I'm not all that interested, so please don't bother'.

And:

Father: Well, what *did* we tell her?

Mother: Well, we told her very early because, well, we had to. And we always spoke very kindly of her other mother. And we told her as much as we were told about her mother — her hobbies, her interests, what she looked like and things like this. But she never even talks about her other mother now, does she? And, again, we don't.

Again:

Mother: She was born in Kent. I have said I feel sorry for her mother. She must always think about her birthday — it must be terrible for her.

Father: We've shown it (the paper) to her. At one time, she seemed interested in knowing more about her mother. And then there was a programme on TV about children having a right to find their parents. And then they showed two people who had found their parents and one was a disaster. She's given us the impression that she's not interested. Whether she really feels differently underneath, I don't know.

Mother: All we have said is that her mother couldn't look after her. She felt it better that she be adopted into another family.

What the parents have withheld

The parents were asked, 'Is there anything that you have felt it best not to tell him/her about his/her first parents and why he/she was adopted?' The parents of 17 of the children said they had not withheld information; three responses were impossible to code. The parents of the remaining 16 children had withheld some information about natural parents, including the existence or siblings of half-siblings, the child's original names, the natural father not knowing about the birth of the child, the occupation of the natural mother and the fact of illegitimacy. For instance, one parent told us:

Mother: Yes. I've glossed over the fact that she's undoubtedly illegitimate because I think that's a lot for a child to have to swallow. I think that what we said was that her mother and father had nowhere to live and rather left it at that. But she doesn't seem very interested.

And others told us:

> *Mother:* Only the fact, I think, that the whole thing was probably a ghastly mistake. And a great embarrassment to all concerned. We haven't actually said that.
> *Father:* No. One tries to soften that.
> *Mother:* I think, in the end, this will become obvious.
> *Father:* I suppose the realisation of this will be gradual and, I suppose, because it's gradual, it's a better way of learning it.

and:

> *Father:* We have her original birth certificate with her original name on it and we've never told her that. We could do if she asked.
> *Mother:* I have a feeling that it would be a very upsetting thing to find out.
> *Father:* To know vaguely that you were adopted is one thing, but to know that you had a different *name* . . .

The most common information withheld (four cases), along with original name, was the existence of natural siblings or half-siblings:

> *Mother:* One I think. The fact that she wasn't the first. I don't think we would ever tell her that; there's no necessity. Maybe it would make her think less of her; I don't know. But that's the only thing we've kept from her.

And:

> *Mother:* The only thing that I haven't really said is that possibly, well, she *has*, she's got half-sisters and brothers. Now and again I've almost said that and then I think perhaps not, let her realise herself. It might set her day-dreaming, mightn't it? I'm going to leave that to her. She might ask later on.

In some instances the parents have withheld, or least not yet mentioned, information which could not have caused the child great difficulty, but which might have been of interest:

> *Interviewer:* Would . . . (child's name) know, for example, that her mother was a nurse?
> *Mother:* No. She's not shown any interest. I nearly mentioned it when one of the teachers said that she was looking after one of the much younger children, and at the time I thought, 'Is this the nurse coming out?'

And:

> *Mother:* We did actually see her father and we didn't tell her that.

What the children know

We asked each of the children, 'Can you tell me about what happened to you

113

as a baby before you came to live with Mum and Dad and . . . (brothers and sisters)?' We coded 11 of the children as having a relatively full knowledge:

Boy: Well, I know a lot because I've read and re-read and re-read and re-read over and over again the letters that were sent to Mum, the confidential letters that were sent to Mum. Mum tends to see that those letters, although they were confidential, they still could, you know, they're still readable to me because they're about me and I still get to know about them. You want me to say what I know?

Interviewer: I'd be interested, yes, if that's OK. But if you don't feel like it . . .

Boy: No, it's all right. That's fine. What I know. I know my original name was . . . That my mother came from Africa and that she wasn't married to my father, whoever he was. That my father was part-Irish — I don't know that either but . . . She left me the ring, a . . . blanket, a thing of soap — I mean a thing of shampoo, soap-dish, which I've got, all of those

Interviewer: Oh, really?

Boy: I've still got that upstairs. I've got things like my baby feeding-sheet, that I was a healthy baby, lively, and that my mother lived with a family or something — I can't remember now. No, I can't quite remember where my mother lived.

Interviewer: Have you got any idea why they were unable to look after you on their own?

Boy: Why she was unable to look after me on her own. Yes, because if she'd have taken me back to Africa, she would have been turned out of the family because that just wouldn't have done within their family sort of thing. Apparently, they're all very, very rich, well, not so much very, very rich as they had a few business stores, things like that, you know. They were very well off, and if she'd have, you know, gone back with me, it would have been awful, and I would have been within that awful situation as well as her. So she wanted me to have a decent life, and she wanted to start afresh in hers so she went back to Africa and I was put on this scheme.

And:

Girl: I can't remember because I was only one, so

Interviewer: Do you know anything about it?

Girl: Um, yes. Um, my mother was white and my father was black. I don't know, I think he came from Africa. And they weren't married, so my mother got pregnant, and I think, I don't really know how old she was — I can't remember — and my father ran back to Africa (laughs) when he heard and I went into a home. But when I was being born, she went (away) because I think she didn't want anybody else to know. And then I was put in a home . . . and that, that's all I know.

Interviewer: Do you know why she didn't feel she was able to look after you?

Girl: I think she was a bit ashamed about it. Well, I think that's why because

114

otherwise I don't know why she'd have gone away to have me, but
Interviewer: Do you know what sort of life they were leading at all?
Girl: I don't really know — oh, except she was good at languages and music, but that's as much as I know about her, really.

Again:

Boy: My real mum wasn't married and she didn't, and she worked in London and her family lived in the country somewhere, and she got pregnant and she didn't want them to know 'cos she wasn't married and she couldn't, she knew, she wouldn't be able to, bring me up, so she adopted me.
Interviewer: I see. So your first mum was living in London, but she didn't come from London. Is that right?
Boy: No. I don't think so. That's . . . Sorry. No, she was working in London and she didn't want her family to know, so I don't even suppose they know now.
Interviewer: Oh, I see. What about your dad? Your first dad. D'you know anything about your first dad or
Boy: I know he was Indian, and he was married and had a family of his own.

Also:

Boy: I do know some things about it that I have been told and I know that my — let's see, I've got to get this right — my father was Indian . . . or something and he came over to England and was a student or something like that. My mother was musical and he — my brain's bad — and I think they got married or something without their real parents knowing, and one of them . . . an arranged marriage or something, something like that. That's what I was told. I was only told quite recently.

One of the responses was impossible to code and the knowledge about natural parents and circumstances of adoption of the remaining 24 appeared to be 'relatively limited'. The following representative comments indicate how limited this knowledge often was:

Girl: No, I don't know much. My mother was Jamaican, and that's about all.
Interviewer: Do you have an idea of details, or do you know any details at all?
Girl: No, no, well, I don't know what Mum and Dad know. I mean, but I know, I suppose, I didn't have a father or . . .

And:

Boy: I was born . . . (abroad) . . . I was then brought to London and put in the adoption home and I was adopted when I was one. And I think that's it, really. Before, that's up to when I was adopted, I don't know any more.
Interviewer: Do you know anything about your first parents? D'you know why they couldn't look after you?

115

Boy: No. I don't know.

Interviewer: Or what they were like?

Boy: I don't really know anything about them, although I'd like to.

Again:

> *Girl:* Mum said that the, um, foster mother — well, all I know is that I was, um, given to this, um, foster mother to look after. It was only about a week or so after I'd been born that I was, you know, put into an adoption home. Then I had a foster mother. And then when I was only a few months old Mum and Dad adopted me. So, really, I'm very lucky; I'm very grateful because I'd have hated to be a child knowing I didn't have parents. I think that would have been really hard. So I'm really glad I was sort of adopted when I was tiny.
>
> *Interviewer:* Do you know anything about your first parents? What they were like? Where they lived? Anything about them at all?
>
> *Girl:* I don't know anything about them *now*. I've nothing, you know, I don't know where they are or anything, but Mum said — I think she said she wasn't quite sure whether they were married or not; . . . I think Mum said she met my mother once, but I don't think she, I don't think she said anything about her. Um, Mum said she sent photographs, a few photographs of me, but that was only when, a few, about a month or so after I was adopted and then I think we haven't really, Mum doesn't even know where they, where my parents are now or anything, you know.

In general, the knowledge that all the children had of their first parents was far from detailed. As many parents pointed out, the subject had not been discussed for some time. And the information described by the children may have been given to them some years ago and not discussed since.

What the children want to know about natural parents

Each child was asked, 'Is there anything you would like to know about your first parents?' The majority of children (25) said there was.

Some children were interested in their parents' lives at the time they (the children) were born.

> *Girl:* I'd just like to find out more about their background and what they did, what they were. Why. But . . . If I thought, maybe if I looked back, it would sort of make me sad, it might make me sad whether I haven't got any regrets. You know? I don't know really. I mean it's not as if I'm unhappy here, anyhow.

And:

> *Girl:* Yeah. I would like to, sort of, um, sort of know what sort of person my mother was like and exactly the sort of situation was. I don't know so much about my

father, but I would like to, interest in what my mother was like, you know? What sort of person she was.

Others were more interested in bringing the story up to date by finding out what their first parents were doing now and in some cases letting the parents see how well their child has turned out:

Interviewer: Are there ever any things that you want, you know, feel that you want to know about them?

Girl: I wouldn't like to meet my father. I don't know why. I just wouldn't but — I suppose in a way I'd quite like to see my mother to see what she's like, and her to see me. I think it'd be nice for her. But I'm not boasting that I'm so marvellous that she'd, but I think she'd quite like to. But I wouldn't really want to chase her because if she'd got married, and hadn't said anything about me, I think it'd be mean, so . . .

And:

Interviewer: Do you ever get curious about them, or wonder about them, or want to know anything about them?

Boy: Yes . . . I wonder where they are, that sort of thing and wonder what their first names were and that sort of thing, and where they're living. But I don't sort of, I only wonder about it when someone brings the subject up. I don't think about it on my own.

Again:

Girl: I'd like to know who they're married to and if they've got any children.

Also:

Boy: I often wonder actually what they were like, or are like. I think — they may be dead now, but if I was told that my original parents were dead, I wouldn't worry a bit because I never knew them so it'd be just like someone I never knew died. I mean, obviously, it would have some effect, sort of, now and again. If they're not still alive, there'd be no point trying to find them. I wanted to, but nothing doing. I mean, I wouldn't sort of, break down on them

Interviewer: Is there anything sort of in particular you'd want to know or

Boy: Well, I would just like to know where they are actually. Where they live . . . I mean, if I had a chance of meeting them, I don't know that I would. I wouldn't know what to sort of react . . . I think it might probably be best for me, actually, being adopted.

The reasons for wanting to know more were not always spelt out, but for some children at least curiosity about themselves had sparked off an interest in their first parents:

117

Interviewer: Is there anything you would like to know about your first mum and dad? I mean is there anything you find yourself wondering about?
Girl: I wonder which one I took after.

And:

Boy: One or two things, yes.
Interviewer: What are the kind of things that you're interested in finding out?
Boy: Well, without wanting to go too far, I wouldn't mind knowing my first mother's name and I wouldn't mind knowing what she looked like, to find out if I, you know, resemble anything like her . . . Dad's got the wrong end of the stick on this one because — I've got to get round to start explaining to him, but, I mean, it's not time yet. He thinks I want to go back to Africa to meet my mother, which I *don't*, because I know if I met my mother, it would cause a lot of conflict and a lot of trouble. So I'd rather go to Africa to see what it was like and to see, you know, from a part of mine, you know, from family origin, if you like. So I'd like to do that, but I wouldn't like to meet her.

Again:

Interviewer: What sort of things would you like to know if it was possible?
Boy: Which one I look like and what they — 'cos I've only got a picture in my mind just that they're my mother and father. I'd like to get a picture of what they *look* like, what they really did look like. But I don't know whether I would ever know that, but it doesn't really worry me.

Several children wanted at some stage to know more, but felt that this was not the appropriate time:

Interviewer: Is there anything more that you would want to know about them, or not at the moment?
Girl: Not at the moment. I think it would bother me to know 'cos I'm too young, really. I'd want to
Interviewer: What? Sort of leave it till a bit later?
Girl: Yes. I, I wouldn't want it to affect me now. Not at this stage.

There were 11 children who said there was nothing more they wanted to know about their first parents. One of these was a child who believed her mother had had a serious accident and was anxious about the conflicting emotions she might feel should she learn any more about her first mother's present life. But the others did not give reasons, and said there was nothing they wanted to know.

Analysing the taped responses of the children who would like further information, we are able to produce the following table:

Table 10.1   What the children wanted to know about their natural parents

Information wanted about natural parents	Number of children
What they looked like	6
Where they live now	4
What work they did	3
What they are doing	• 2
Their first names	2
Why they couldn't keep me	2
Which one I take after	2
How old they were	1
What they were good at	1
What they were like	1
My real name	1
Where I was living	1
What she's like	1
Who they're married to and if they have children	1
Total number of children wanting information	25*

* *Some children wanted more than one item of information*

Of the children who said they would like more information about their first parents or some contact with them, the majority were previously described as initiating discussion about adoption with their parents if and when they wanted to. Presumably, however, they felt unable or unwilling to discuss these subjects with their adoptive parents or at least, if they had discussed them, they had not obtained answers. In reviewing the list of items mentioned, however, many would clearly not be known by the adoptive parents.

Summary

In this chapter we have examined how the issue of adoption is dealt with in the family and whether the children's needs for discussion and knowledge are met. Although we are dealing with a group of transracially-adopted children, our findings have relevance for other families with adopted teenage children.

119

Although, by the time the children had reached their teens, adoption seemed to be discussed only infrequently within the family, there was no general confusion about whose role it was to initiate such discussions. Most of the families seemed to have come to an agreement that it is the role of either the parents or the child to initiate conversations. We could find only limited evidence of family systems in which both parents and children were each expecting the other to initiate discussions.

However, when it comes to analysing what the parents talk about and what the children want to know, there is evidence that for some children their interest and need for information was not being met. Admittedly, a lot of the information that the children would be interested in obtaining is not known by the parents, but at the same time, some parents did not seem to realise what information their children would like to have. Although the parents might not know the precise information required, some conversations about the general areas of interest might have been valuable.

What impressed us was that, although the channels of communication about adoption were there (e.g., in terms of agreement about who initiates conversations), there seemed to be some reluctance to use these channels. The parents were sometimes reluctant to discuss adoption and to give specific information because the child would be upset. The children at the same time did not want to seem disloyal and to upset their parents by too much discussion or by displaying interest in specific aspects of their natural parentage. The evidence presented at the beginning of the chapter about lack of contact with other families in a similar position may be related to this. Possibly conversations are that much easier if adoptive families are in touch with other families in a similar position.

This had not caused serious problems for the children, as their relationships inside and outside the home indicate. Whether the issues surrounding adoption will become even more significant in the later teenage years remains to be seen. There may be a point at which somehow the family must reconcile their need to keep fast their bonds, with the adoptee's need to build her own life by reclaiming the fragments she has lost.

11

The black and mixed-race adopters

Previous chapters have concentrated on the 36 BAP families who have adopted transracially. In the original group there were, however, a number of black or mixed-race couples who adopted children and eight of these families were seen for the present study. Although these eight families cannot be regarded as a control group, they do provide an interesting comparison with the 36 families in the main group. This is particularly the case because same-race placements are increasingly regarded as the ideal by social workers. However, because of the small number of black same-race placements that have been made in this country, there is as yet little evidence on the outcome of such placements.

Methodology

The procedure for interviewing the black and mixed-race couples and the method of coding the material was the same as for the transracial adopters. Some questions were omitted from the original interview schedule and others were altered. The large majority of the questions was identical.

As with the main group, the intention was to interview the parents together prior to seeing the child on her own. In the event, three fathers were unable to be present due to work demands. In one case the mother reluctantly agreed to be interviewed on her own, but refused permission for the child to be interviewed or for his school to be contacted.

In three cases, although the child was interviewed, the parents did not give permission to contact the school. For this reason the information we did obtain from the schools is described only when it is relevant to a particular child.

The eight families

The group contains four boys and four girls; five are mixed-race in that they had one white natural parent. In three of the adoptive couples both partners are black, whilst in the remaining five couples the mothers are white. Information on the families is summarised in Table 11.1.

121

Table 11.1 **Details of black and mixed-race adoptive families**

Family	Adoptive mother	Adoptive father	Boy's racial background	Girl's racial background
1	West Indian	West Indian	West Indian/ West Indian	
2	Trinidadian	Trinidadian		White/ West Indian
3	Guyanese	Guyanese	White/ West Indian	
4	White	African		White/ West Indian
5	White	Ceylonese		Indian/ Singhalese
6	White	African	White/ West Indian	
7	White	Indian		Thai/Iraqi
8	White	Indian	White/ Indian	

None of the eight couples had been divorced, although one had suffered serious marital problems over a number of years and was, at the time of the study, planning legal separation.

The families were all buying their own homes in London or surrounding counties. Interestingly, their neighbourhoods and the catchment areas of the children's schools were predominantly white, although two had a significant black population.

Also, the children reported having a primarily white circle of friends. One child had no black friends and three had only one. Only one of the seven children interviewed talked of having a mixed group of friends.

All but one of the mothers worked outside the home, part-time or full-time. Of the seven fathers on whom we have employment information, three were in skilled manual jobs and the remaining four were in non-manual jobs.

Four of the couples had an additional child apart from the study child, but two was the maximum family size. Two of those couples had a child of their marriage before adopting, and two adopted a younger child after the BAP adoption. The large proportion of couples with no children of their marriage (six), the number of single children (four) and the maximum size of the families (two children) is in contrast to the group of transracial adopters.

None of the eight families had any serious health problems.

Relationships within the family

Parents' descriptions of their children were generally positive. The parents of one child with serious behaviour and academic problems expressed understandable concern about his adjustment. He had been expelled from two schools. Although the parents were open about their son's quite serious problems, they nevertheless conveyed warmth and concern for him and described their relationship with him in basically positive terms.

The children were also very positive about their parents and about relationships within the family. Their responses indicated that they saw the family as a source of support and close relations, and scores on the family integration scale confirm this. As with the transracially-adopted children, they sometimes found it difficult to put into words what their parents were like as people or what the parents thought of them, but in general we received a consistent picture of positive relationships.

Relationships outside the family

As with the main group, we attempted to examine their ability to form relationships outside the home and how they got on at school. We were handicapped, however, by having no school reports on four of the children and by being unable to interview one of the children.

The eight mothers and five fathers with whom we talked gave positive descriptions of their children's peer relationships. When the children were asked about their friends, relationships seemed generally to be good, although two of them expressed some difficulties. A third child described having good friends in a 'bad crowd' known for its delinquent behaviour. The four school reports we received confirmed the views of both parents and children.

Academic progress

The parents were happy or mainly happy with their children's progress at school, with the exception of the couple whose son had been expelled. They described their children's ability as average or above average with the same single exception.

Racial background: policies and experiences

Family and school life seemed happy and satisfactory for all but one of this sub-group of children. We now deal in more detail with how racial background has been coped with and experienced in these families. We do this because the assumption of many social workers is that it is in the black or mixed-race family that the child will develop a positive sense of racial identity.

The same areas were covered regarding policies towards bringing up a black child as had been covered with the white adopters. Four of the eight couples or parents interviewed said they had an entirely white or predominantly white circle of friends; only one said that the majority of their friends was black.

Of the eight mothers and five fathers we interviewed, only one mother said she had made very positive attempts to give her child a sense of identity with his racial background. The following is part of this black mother's response to the 'policy' question:

> *Mother:* And so they should take us and be proud of us for what we are and they should be proud of us to know that we are pushing them on to have a better life and to have a better education more than what we have. They should be proud of us. And in a way they should be proud of the people, proud of themselves in the country, and they should want to do everything in their power for both sides, whether European or whether coloured that the country should be a better country, for them in later years.

Two other couples said that they had made some attempt to encourage the child to identify with her racial background, but the remainder had no specific approach or, as with the parents of two children, were raising the child 'as if she was white'.

The following quotes from an English mother and Indian father illustrate this:

> *Interviewer:* But do you feel that you need to give her some sort of pride in her Indian or her . . .
> *Father:* No . . . The only pride that I can give her is to be a human being. That's all.
> *Interviewer:* So, really her identity's here rather than . . .
> *Father:* Yes.
> *Mother:* Well, I think she really thinks of herself as English because she's sort of gone to an English school and . . .
> *Father:* She (was) born in England. So . . .

There is, of course, a possibility that the family's stated policy may differ from the general atmosphere created within the family. This was illustrated by one father who said he had no specific approach on this subject, but throughout the interview there were references to the West Indies, to West Indians who excelled in sport, and to the extended family still living 'at home'.

One important aspect of the parents' attitudes towards racial background is their view of the position of blacks in Britain. When parents were asked whether they thought their child had to do better at school than a white child to have the same chances in life, responses were mixed. Some couples answered, 'yes':

> *Father:* Well, I would think so. Well, *I've* had to do more than another white worker to, to just survive really, and I think the same thing would apply to him or any coloured child in that respect.
>
> *Mother:* No, I think that it's, um, a natural thing. It's you've got to be born. No one can visualise what it is or the pressures of being coloured unless you *are* coloured. You've got to be born coloured to know what the pressures are. But you see, . . . you know from the time that you're growing up — this is a *dis*advantage that we find with kids in this country. Because, you see, in our own country we haven't got this racial problem; there's no pressure. But you accept the fact that when you come . . .

And:

> *Father:* Economic climate or not, it has always been my opinion that you don't have to be as good as, you have to be better than . . . Perhaps that might sort of be the icing on the cake, if you like. But very important — yes, it is a fact, they have to be better.
>
> *Interviewer:* Is that something that concerns you, too? Or is it something you're aware of with her school work and that you encourage in particular?
>
> *Mother:* Yes. I am aware of that. Sort of, when she goes outside, you know, you sort of will expect this . . . She would come up against it outside.

All the parents said they thought black youngsters faced problems in this country, including difficulties in getting a job, police harassment and a general lack of acceptance:

> *Father:* Being accepted. And getting jobs. I would say so. Being accepted. And after a while they develop this defence mechanism of being aggressive, etc. and it's natural. I mean, I've done it before when I was younger. But I would say, being accepted. I think the darker they are, the worse it is.

One additional point, raised by a black mother, illustrates the dilemma of black youngsters born in this country:

> *Mother:* They were born here; they have no other culture besides what they learn

here. They have no other background and all they can see is the people around them. And in this sense they find it more difficult than we do. Because we can always fall back on the past — but they have nowhere to go. And I think this is the problem here with black kids who were born in this country. They haven't got roots. And this is what makes them so bitter, because they are not accepted *as part* of Britain and they have nothing to identify themselves with except Britain . . . They're not English and the blacks don't, um — if you speak with a Cockney accent to an average West Indian, he'll, 'Oh, well, look at him. He's just, he's neither here or there. He's not one of us and not one of them, so what is he? He's nothing.'

How the children see themselves

When asked to describe their appearance for someone who is meeting them for the first time only two of the children referred to their racial background. Both of these were boys; one described himself as 'coloured' and the other as 'half-caste'.

As with the transracially-adopted children, none of the sub-group children used the term 'black' when referring to their racial background. For two of the seven children there was no regular description in use; two said 'coloured'; one said 'coloured and half-caste'; one said 'half-caste' and one said she thought of herself as 'Jamaican', but would describe herself as 'English' to other people.

Although all of the parents said they thought black youngsters in Britain faced considerable difficulties, the children were not unanimous in their equivalent responses. Most felt there were difficulties, but were unable to be very specific. For example:

Boy: Sometimes it's because of their colour; sometimes it's themselves.
Interviewer: What sort of problems do you think crop up?
Boy: Oh, it all depends.
Interviewer: Do you think it's hard to get on in this country?
Boy: Not really.

This boy's response is in contrast to the views of his parents who gave long, articulate descriptions of the problems they and their friends had encountered.

Only one child referred to a specific incident to back up her response:

Girl: Hurting them, um, being cruel to them because of their colour.
Interviewer: Do you mean saying things or actually doing violence?
Girl: Well, saying things and being violent to them. My Mum's friend at work, her daughter in . . . pushed her head in the toilet because she came from India . . .

Yes. And the girl didn't do anything. The mother said, 'Well, I'm not going to stick up for you if you're not going to fight back.' So then, the next time they hurt her, she bashed one of the girls' head against the wall and it cracked so . . .

When we asked the seven children to tick one of the three statements about orientation to colour, none answered, 'I am proud to be coloured/black/brown'; six answered, 'I don't really mind what colour I am', and one answered, 'I would prefer to be white'.

Most of the children said they were not interested in learning more about West Indian/Asian/African life, but if they did want information, parents, television and newspapers were seen as the main sources. Only two of the children said they wanted in future to live in the way they thought Asians/West Indians/Africans lived, although some did say they hoped to have more contact with black people in future.

One rather sad comment illustrates the distance from the black community felt by one boy:

Interviewer: When you're older and leave home, would you like to spend more time with Indian people, or not?

Boy: Well, I wouldn't do it by choice . . . but I wouldn't mind if I had to, if it was a job, if it was my job, then I wouldn't really care.

Self-esteem

The seven children's scores on the Coopersmith inventory ranged from 50 to 93, with a mean score of 76. This mean score is slightly lower than for the transracially adopted children, but still appears to indicate that the children are experiencing no general difficulties.

Being black in a white society

The children were asked how it felt to be 'black/brown/coloured' in a white society. All but one said it did not cause problems; the other said:

Boy: Some people aren't sure. They say, 'Are you white or are you black?' You know, they say, 'What are you? Where d'you come from?'

Interviewer: D'you get a lot of that?

Boy: Oh yes. A lot . . . But, actually, as I try and stay in the background — I don't push myself forward, I don't, I don't really, you know, if there's, I try and stay out of kids' way, you see . . . Well, I don't really think of myself as being coloured, sort of being brought up with a white parent and a black parent, though my Dad isn't really as close to me as my Mum. He loves me just as much,

127

but — I think I'm closer to my Mum, having been brought up — I haven't got an accent . . . I go around with white kids. I haven't really had . . . black friends at all so I've been brought up really in a white society.

When asked directly about unpleasant experiences related to colour (anyone being nasty, etc.), name-calling was most frequently mentioned.

Being adopted

Five of the seven children interviewed said they started conversations about adoption or at least would do so if they wanted to. One said she waited, and another said that she did not want to know anything more, so it was not relevant. Once again, the infrequency with which the subject arose was commented on by both parents and children. Generally, the parents appeared to give the children only limited details, with the parents of four children saying they have withheld some facts.

One feature of the responses on this topic, as with the transracially-adopted group, was how uniformly little the children were able to recall about their backgrounds. The following is an example:

Interviewer: Do you ever think at all about your first mum and dad or any of that or are you not really sort of bothered about all that?
Girl: Not really — because I love my Mum and Dad that I've got now
Interviewer: So you don't sort of think . . .
Girl: No. I don't start worrying . . .
Interviewer: So is there anything at all that you ever want to know about them or . . .?
Girl: Well, I know just what I know because we've got a piece of paper upstairs that we got from the adoption people and my feeding things and that we had. And it tells me what colour hands they had, what colouring and that and that's all I really need to know.

Summary

The current socialwork emphasis on same-race placements is not based on the monitored outcome of such placements. The responses from these eight families should shed a little light on issues and experiences which clearly need much more investigation. Although these eight families cannot in any way be regarded as a control group, the results do hint at interesting comparisons with the main group of families who have adopted transracially.

The first point that emerges is that these adoptions, as with the transracial adoptions, seem to have been on the whole successful from the perspective of both parents and children.

128

In terms of racial background, the data presented in this chapter hint at a number of significant issues. First, although the children have more opportunity for contact with black adults and children than their transracially adopted counterparts, for the most part the children live not only in a white-dominated society, they also reside in, socialise in and are educated in a predominantly white environment. The parents' occupational status and place in the housing market is perhaps more significant in determining this environment than their racial background.

Second, although the parents themselves tend to be articulate about the problems of blacks in this country, for the most part they do not have a policy of stressing racial pride or identity. Related to this is the indication that the children do not seem positively to identify with the black community, nor do they appear to express a sense of racial pride. There is no indication, however, that this is a general source of difficulty or confusion for the children; the responses related to family life and self-esteem are roughly equivalent to those in the other group.

Finally, as with the transracial group, adoption is not frequently discussed and most of the parents give only limited accounts to the child. Although these families might be expected to be generally more familiar with the origins and cultures of the black natural parents, the children are not given any more details than their transracially adopted counterparts.

Again, it must be stressed that no firm conclusions can be based on a small group of this size. But the results of our interviews with these eight families alert us to treat with caution the assumption that children placed with black or mixed-race couples will necessarily come to develop a strong identity based on racial background and that their experience of their 'colour' or racial background will automatically be less problematic than that of their transracially adopted counterparts.

12

Conclusions and policy implications

In this book we have examined the lives and experiences of transracially adopted children who have reached adolescence. We have also related their lives and experiences to the approaches and philosophies of their parents and to the reactions of the wider communities in which the children have been growing up. In particular, we have attempted to see how racial background has been defined and dealt with inside the families and have explored the links between these definitions and policies and those used in the wider society.

In summarising our findings we again keep to the distinction between the 36 children in the BAP group who are transracially adopted and those adopted by couples in which one or both partners is black or mixed-race.

First, we found no general evidence of the children being isolated within their families. Close and intimate family relations had developed for the large majority of the children. The children saw themselves as 'belonging to this family'.

Second, in spite of their often having very little contact with other children of the same racial background, we found that the large majority of children were able to relate effectively to peers and adults outside the family. Also, there is no evidence of the children doing worse academically than their age-mates: if anything, the study children seemed to be doing better.

When analysing issues related to racial background we found that the large majority of parents had made only limited or very limited attempts to give their children a sense of racial pride and awareness of their racial origin. The children in turn saw themselves as 'white' in all but skin colour and had little knowledge or experience of their counterparts growing up in the black community.

There was no general evidence, however, that the absence of racial pride or identity was, at this stage, associated with low self-esteem or behavioural disorder. If there was a degree of 'identity confusion', there was nothing to suggest that this was experienced as significantly problematic by the children or that it was associated with a poor self-concept and low self-esteem.

The majority of the children could describe unpleasant or distressing incidents related to how others had reacted to their racial background and yet for the large majority this did not appear to be experienced as a central aspect of their lives. Also, when talking about the time at which racial background was most significant, both parents and children tended to talk about the period earlier than adolescence when the children were starting in their first schools.

On the distinction between the black and mixed-race children, we found no evidence that the experience of racial background had been clearly different. The families seemed to have reacted similarly to both groups of children. The children themselves did not appear to have consistently different views about the significance of their racial background.

These, then, are the main findings, and on the basis of the evidence presented in this study we can find little support for the criticisms of transracial adoption which are based on the anticipated difficulties of the child. The only potential criticism we have been unable to examine is the final one — that being brought up in white society transracially adopted children will not be able to relate to members of the black community. As yet the majority of the BAP children have not been in a position where such contact is a possibility.

In terms of what could be regarded as four crucial measures of outcome (*relationships within the family, peer-group relationships, level of self-esteem* and *behavioural disorders*) the research suggests that only a small number of these adoptions can be regarded as problematic. Combining the evidence on these areas of our research, we conclude that there is evidence of some difficulties in the lives of five of the boys and one of the girls. Two of these children are mixed-race. Again, it must be stressed that this assessment, as with all such assessments, is somewhat subjective, but we base it on problematic responses in at least two of these areas. The children causing different degrees of concern are:

Boy No. 1   Low 'family cohesion' score and describes some difficulties in peer-group relations.

Boy No. 2   Defines father negatively; school says he is below average in popularity; receives problematic score on both the parents' and teachers' Rutter scales.

Boy No. 3   Parents and child describe problems in relationships; parents and child describe difficulties in peer-group relations; receives problematic score on both the teachers' and parents' Rutter scales.

Boy No. 4   Parents and child define problems with relationship; child

131

describes some difficulties in relation to peers; child scores low on Coopersmith self-esteem inventory (49).

Boy No. 5 School defines child as below average in popularity and he receives a problematic score on the teachers' Rutter scale.

Girl No. 1 School says she is below average in popularity; receives problematic score on teachers' and parents' Rutter scales.

These, then, are the six children out of the 36 for whom the picture is perhaps a less happy one. It should, however, be noted that the range of difficulties is wide. For instance, one boy (No. 3) is experiencing considerable difficulties on a majority of responses, whereas for another (No. 5) there is only evidence from the school that he experiences difficulty; and such inconsistency between school and family is of course open to different interpretations.

It should be remembered, however that the children causing concern represent only 17 per cent of the transracially adopted group and in only one case has there ever been any indication of a breakdown in the adoption. And in some ways the adjustments that this 17 per cent of the children and their families have made have been successful.

It is fair to regard the rest of these adoptions as definitely 'successful'. This is consistent with what is known of the 'success' of adoptions in which different racial background has not been a factor. For instance, in a review of adoption studies carried out between 1924 and 1968 by 15 different researchers, Kadushin concluded that 74 per cent were 'unequivocally successful', and 15 per cent were 'unsuccessful', 'unsatisfactory', 'poor' or 'problematic'. The remaining 11 fell in an intermediate group.[1]

The way we have assessed outcome is different from that used in the previous follow-up study in that we have been able to base our assessments in part on what the children have told us. It is difficult, therefore, to make a direct comparison. However, there does seem to be consistency between the ratings given at that time and our assessments. In the 1975 follow-up, four children were giving cause for concern in that either the child or the family's adjustment was regarded as poor. Of these four children, two are in our group of six (Boys No. 2 and 3), one was not in our sample and the fourth, a girl, was in our sample, but seems to be doing well at the moment. Interestingly, her parents talked about how things had 'much improved'.

The evidence from our study, therefore, is that a small proportion of the children do have difficulties. But we feel confident in using the term 'success' to describe the experiences of the majority of these families and children. And there is little evidence that a group of similarly-aged white children growing up with their natural parents would not include a number of children experiencing similar or greater difficulties than those of the study children.

Possible reasons for 'success'

The most obvious reason for the successful outcome of these adoptions is the commitment and caring of the adoptive parents. Although we came across families living in different settings and developing different family styles, we were impressed by the natural and continuing dedication to make *this* child part of *this* family. Their philosophies had been that the child should be regarded, cared for and loved in the same way as their natural children.

A number of other factors are, however, also significant. All of the children in the BAP group had been placed when they were very young. In effect, this meant that the children had grown up entirely in a white world. Except in their very early months, all of the significant people in their lives had been white. They had grown up in a world in which, although racial background might have been underplayed or in some cases ignored, the messages and definitions about their racial background had at least been consistent.

The third factor which we consider to be of significance in interpreting our findings concerns the nature of the children's lives as they enter adolescence. In talking to the BAP children we were left with the impression that they often considered other things more important than the colour of their skin. They were living in a world which was full of the challenges and dilemmas of adolescence. Success at school, the beginnings of anticipation of jobs and careers, success with friends, success at sport and hobbies, in all but a few cases seemed more central concerns than the children's racial background. We had anticipated that racial background would be a crucial determinant of the children's experience of their world. What we found was not that it was insignificant — the incidents and descriptions used in this study do not support that conclusion — but that for the majority other issues were more important. Rephrasing this finding into the vocabulary of 'identity', the children were faced with a wide variety of identity material of which racial background was rarely reported as the most important.

The fourth significant factor in understanding our findings is the class nature of adoption. In the United States Mandell has argued that

a class analysis of adoption and foster care will pinpoint the problems of the systems more precisely than does a purely psychological analysis of individual

133

motivation and personality dynamics or an analysis of role relationships divorced from a view of the larger social system.[2]

In this country Holman has taken up the same theme and argued that

in evaluating outcomes, adoption investigations may confuse the effects of class with that of adoption.[3]

The results presented in our study lend themselves to analysis along the lines of Mandell and Holman. First, because of their class position and, related to this, their position in the housing market, the large majority of the BAP families are living in areas far removed from the racially-mixed neighbourhoods of our large cities. In terms of the children's experience of their racial background this means that they are living in areas in which racial tension is not likely to be a factor. Indeed, as we showed in Chapter 6, there was by no means agreement among the parents that living in racially-mixed areas was likely to be an advantage to their children. Some parents assessed the dangers of racial tension associated with living in such areas as more than outweighing the possible advantages of being in contact with other black or mixed-race children. Living far away from the centres of ethnic minority residence also has a possible advantage in terms of family integration; definitions of, and significance attached to, racial background in the families were not challenged.

Related to this, the majority of the children are growing up in families which are likely, because of their geographical and financial position, to provide their children with schooling which in turn will provide them with qualifications necessary to make a successful transition from school to work. One common statement during the parents' interviews was, 'No, he/she will not face difficulties related to colour because of his/her qualifications/achievements'. Rephrasing this in class terms, what the parents are saying is that because of all the advantages of a middle-class education and upbringing their children are avoiding some of the problems normally associated with ethnic minority status — lack of qualifications and no power in the job market.

This interpretation of the importance of class was reinforced during our interviews with the children. We were struck by how frequently the statements they made about their own-race contemporaries growing up in their own community were in fact statements based on assumptions of the *class* position of these contemporaries. Statements relating to difficulty in finding work and lack of money are clearly statements not about *culture*, but about *class*.

Obviously we cannot come to firm conclusions about the impact of class

134

upon the success of the BAP placements. Such conclusions could only be drawn following a study which incorporated control groups of transracially-adopted children growing up in racially-mixed areas and children adopted by families who were less able to give them the advantages of a middle-class education. Yet a class analysis seems of central importance in interpreting some of our findings and explaining how the parents and children perceived their position.

Policies for the future

The BAP group has to be seen in its historical context. They adopted their children at a particular stage of the history of 'race relations' in this country. They adopted their children when, far from placing black children in black homes, the adoption agencies were considered to be advanced if they found white homes for such children. What were then regarded as placements which challenged the status quo are now regarded by many social workers as traditional and discriminatory.

Understanding the state of thinking current in the agencies at that time, it seems fair to argue that transracial adoption was a necessary and important stage in agency policy. It was a stage that eventually led on to the situation we have today, where black homes for black children are a very real possibility.

Also it must be remembered that if transracial adoptions had not been considered for children such as the BAP group, then the likely alternatives for these children at that time would have been growing up in care. And again, given the situation at the time, and as now, that would have meant possibly a fluctuating career between white children's homes and white foster homes.

Given this historical perspective on transracial adoption and given that such placements have offered a family environment for many black children, we must surely welcome the finding of our study that the children appear to be doing well at the present time. Also, the BAP group is amongst the oldest group of transracially-adopted children in this country and our findings are of significance for those families with younger children who have been placed in this way. They are significant in terms of indicating the various pressures that the children have experienced at different stages in their lives. They are significant in terms of indicating some of the ways in which the children have 'coped' with their situation. And they are significant in terms of indicating that the children themselves might at this age be now desiring some more conversations and information about their origins.

Also, we would argue that our findings are of relevance for more recent

135

transracial placements in which the children are perhaps more likely to have been West Indian rather than Asian. The central questions posed for the adoptive families remain the same — the nature of integration into the family, the possibility of developing a positive racial identity and the fact that different racial backgrounds highlight the fact of adoption. Obviously, the realities of racial prejudice may be different for different groups, but the central characteristics of the families created by such adoptions remain the same.

In spite of our findings of 'success' at this stage, question marks still of course remain in relation to the BAP group and will continue to do so for some years in the future. Perhaps the most important of these is how the children will fare as they increasingly move out of their family and home environments and have to come to terms more directly with life in a society where many people will characterise them on the basis of their racial background. They will be moving out into a society which is significantly racist in its attitudes and its distribution of opportunities. They will be moving towards establishing their own families, and racial background will be an issue.

It is very tempting on the basis of our findings to say that the care, attention and feelings of self-worth they have been given will see them through. And yet the question still remains as to whether these undoubted advantages will be enough. What seems certain is that racial background will become more significant in the coming years for some of these children. They will come to understand something of the circumstances of their placement in white families and something of the way in which racial background is defined. We are reminded of the 17-year-old transracially-adopted boy to whom we talked at the pilot stage of our research, who told us that he used to think of himself as 'coloured', but now he thought of himself as 'black'.

Although the families feel a sense of optimism, and the research evidence largely supports this, our research can offer no definite predictions on the future of these children and the issues that will be raised by their racial background. We do not know whether the 'coping techniques' they have learnt within the context of their strong white families will be adequate when they move into adult life. Listening to the children talk about how they cope, it is apparent that methods and tactics are typically related more to their successfully denying racial background than seeing it as a source of positive strength. And we do not know how significant this lack of a strong racial identity will be as they negotiate the stages ahead.

These questions about the future of the BAP group relate directly to what can be considered one of the main issues presented by our study — the difficulty for the black child of developing a sense of racial identity in the white family. The reasons for this as we have indicated are, first, the tensions between making the child fully part of the family and at the same time highlighting her differences. Second, they are that because of their class and related position in the housing market the families seem unlikely to have significant contacts with the black community. At one level therefore this study, although pointing to 'success' by conventional criteria, has highlighted and underlined some of the fears of the critics of transracial adoption. These black children have been made white in all but skin colour. They have no contact with the black community. Their 'coping' mechanisms are based on denying their racial background.

But although we have described the experiences of the BAP group in detail, other factors have to be considered in terms of policies for the future. How black children have 'fared' in adoption is only one of the questions that have to be asked. In assessing other factors we are drawn back to the distinction that was made in the first chapter between (a) criticisms of transracial adoption based on the anticipated experiences of a black child in a white family and (b) criticisms based on discrimination against the black community. Our research was based on the first category of criticisms, but it is the second category which perhaps deserves more attention at the present time.

Transracial adoption over the past two decades has illustrated and highlighted the disadvantages of blacks in white society. To understand this it is necessary to examine the pressures that have led to a disproportionate number of black children being made available for adoption and a disproportionate number of black children being taken into care. Not only have black families suffered from the material hardship which is likely to produce pressures and tensions in child-care, but also white welfare agencies have in many cases developed a stigmatising view of the character and capacities of the black family. And this view, it can be argued, has been partly instrumental in producing the large number of black children received into care. The black community has every justification for seeing itself as a 'donor' of children for white couples. Such a perception can do little for the dignity and self-determination of that community. To have a system which through 'benign neglect' in effect systematically removes black children from black homes and places them in white homes without any traffic in the opposite direction can hardly be beneficial for the black community.

In talking about transracial adoption we are therefore drawn back into the widescale issues of the distribution of resources and the distribution of opportunities. A discussion of how the children have 'fared' in adoption is for these reasons only limited and partial.

137

The arguments that were first heard more than a decade ago in North America are now therefore being more forcefully put in this country. These arguments, as we indicated at the beginning of this book, are that transracial adoption, through the mechanisms of the 'adoption market' has represented the traditional servicing of whites by blacks, in this context by providing children for them. Secondly, that transracial placements take from the black community what must be seen as ultimately their most valuable resource — their children. And, third, that the black community cannot hope to maintain its pride and dignity if advantage is defined for them by these placements as being brought up by white families. Somehow, on these grounds alone, the impetus for finding black homes has to be maintained and increased.

There are also very important practical reasons for greater effort being put into the search for black homes. The first of these is that there are now many more older black children for whom adoption is a real possibility. Our research was based on children who were placed when very young. But it is possible that older black children may by the time a placement has occurred have already internalised a definition of themselves as being black and that this definition may jeopardise the possibility of integration and emotional identification within a white family.

The second intensely practical reason why black homes for black children must become a reality is that there is now some evidence of the black natural parents only being willing for their children to be adopted by black families. If this desire becomes more widespread, as indeed it could, then the failure of some agencies to recruit black adoptive parents could have a particularly damaging effect on some children.

Finding more black adoptive families will necessitate more black social workers in the key agency posts that determine policy, more black social workers involved in family-finding and child-placement, and increased sensitivities on the part of social workers in general to the strengths of the black community as providers of alternative families. Already some imaginative attempts have been made to find these parents from the black community. The Soul Kids Campaign pioneered attempts to find black homes for black children in this country.[3] More recently, in 1980, the New Black Families Unit was set up in London by Lambeth Social Services and the Independent Adoption Society.[4]

More generally, there is now evidence that white social workers in different agencies in different parts of the country are now taking much more seriously the argument that it is the right of every black child to grow up in his or her own community. As a result of this belief, although transracial placements are still being made, more active steps are being taken to seek out new black adopters and to move away from the traditional conceptions of what makes a suitable adoptive home. These initiatives, like the more publicised ones, are crucial and we hope they will mark major increases in the number of black families providing alternative family care. They are also part of a wider movement in social work to provide a service which is sensitive to the needs of different ethnic minorities.

The challenge for policy makers now seems to be to recognise the immediate needs of individual children while at the same time developing a comprehensive service which is sensitive both to the needs and strengths of the black community. We believe that it is vitally important for every effort to be made to find black homes for black children wherever possible, but we must be realistic. Now, and for some time to come, unless some black children are to remain indefinitely in public care and be denied the benefits of any kind of family, some transracial placements will need to be made. It is hoped that in arranging such placements proper attention will be paid to the willingness and capacity of the families to enable the black child to establish and maintain contact with the black community and to develop a real sense of his own racial identity and heritage.

In conclusion, our research findings have to be seen in the light of historical developments. The arguments are now not about whether placement in a black or white family is more appropriate, but about how more black families can be encouraged to adopt. The purpose of this book has been to review and evaluate a form of placement which has provided families for many black children over the last two decades. By and large, using conventional measures of adoption success, the children in the placements studied appeared to be doing well. They did not, however, see themselves as black or show any real sign of having developed a sense of racial identity. These findings will be assessed and weighted by different readers in different ways. However, it is no part of our intention, in concluding, to advocate either a return to the period when transracial adoption was the norm; or to criticise transracial adoption in such a way that mixed race families and their children become pawns in the current arguments for same-race placements. It is not necessary to imply that the many children who have been adopted transracially are suffering major difficulties in order for us to support the call for same-race placements. Indeed, to prejudge the issue could have the dangerous consequence of becoming a self-fulfilling prophecy. Nevertheless, in our view, there are strong arguments for saying that wherever possible black children needing a permanent substitute home should be placed in black rather than white families. But, there are large numbers of black children in urgent and immediate need of the security and love of a family, and it is clear that at least in the short term, transracial adoption, whatever its disadvantages or its strengths, will continue to play a part in meeting that need.

Postscript: *the future*

Wherever possible in this study we have let the families speak for themselves. It therefore seems appropriate that we should allow the parents the final word about the future. The parents of all but two of the 36 children felt general confidence about the future of their children, although, when asked, 20 said they anticipated some specific difficulties related to racial background:

> *Mother:* She's as well equipped as anyone could be to cope with her situation, I think. Both temperamentally and in terms of her experience and confidence, which has grown enormously over her secondary period.

> *Father:* Oh, I think you can foresee *possible* difficulties in the sense that she's not obviously going to get ten Grade A O-levels or anything like that. In fact, she'll be lucky if she gets more than one or two, but that doesn't mean to say that she can't get an interesting, well-paid job and enjoy herself.

> *Mother:* We just wonder about marriage — that's the one thing . . . because that could make, you know, so much — might meet some nice, absolutely white young man whose parents might find this very difficult.

> *Mother:* I feel quite confident. She'll make it. Intellectually she'll have no problems. She'll probably go to university. She'll probably get a job fairly easily unless there are long queues . . . As a person, she can cope quite adequately, I would say, with life. She can hold her own.

As with many parents at the present time, the BAP group express anxiety about their children's future employment. Added to this, there are a number of specific issues relating to racial background which cause some anxiety. But the general view is an optimistic one. The children will make it.

References and Notes

Chapter 1

1 Simon, R.J. and Altstein, H., *Transracial Adoption*, John Wiley, 1977.
2 *ibid.*, pp. 10–11.
3 *ibid.*, p. 4.
4 Jones, E.D., 'On transracial adoption of black children', *Child Welfare* 51(3), 1972, pp. 156–64.
5 Chestang, L., 'The dilemma of biracial adoption', *Social Work* (USA), May 1972, pp. 100–101.
6 Child Welfare League of America, *Standards for Adoption Service*, p. 92, quoted in Day, D., *The Adoption of Black Children*, D.C. Heath, 1979.
7 For discussion of this and reports of a project that had some success see *The Soul Kids Campaign*, Association of British Adoption and Fostering Agencies, 1976.
8 Fitzgerald, J., 'Black parents for black children', *Adoption and Fostering*, no. 103, 1981, p. 10.
9 James, M., 'Finding the families', *Adoption and Fostering*, no. 103, 1981, p. 12.
10 For instance, Benet refers to Ben Finley, founder of Chicago's Afro-American Family and Community Services, who regarded the 'crowning irony' as being that white people had throughout the history of the United States used black people to raise their children; now they were denying them the opportunity to raise their own. Benet, M.K., *The Character of Adoption*, Jonathan Cape, 1976.
11 Fanshel, D., *Far from the Reservation: the transracial adoption of American Indian children*, Scarecrow Press, 1972.
12 Grow, L.C. and Shapiro, D., *Black Children, White Parents: a study of transracial adoption*, Child Welfare League of America, 1974.
13 Chimezie, A., 'Bold but irrelevant: Grow and Shapiro on transracial adoption', *Child Welfare*, Vol. 56, February 1977, pp. 75–86.
14 Simon, R.J. and Altstein, H., *op.cit.*
15 *ibid.*, p. 130.
16 Simon, R.J. and Altstein, H., *Transracial Adoption: a follow-up*, Lexington Books, 1981.
17 Kim, D.S., 'Intercountry Adoptions: a study of self-concept of adolescent Korean children who were adopted by American families'. Unpublished Ph.D. thesis, University of Chicago, 1976. Referred to in *Social Work Research Abstracts*, National Association of Social Workers, and also referred to by Maas, H.S., *Social Service Research*, NASW, Washington, DC, 1978.
18 For details of the original project, see: Raynor, L., *Adoption of Non-White Children in Britain*, Allen and Unwin, 1970.
19 *ibid.*

20 Jackson, B., *Family Experiences of Inter-Racial Adoption*, Association of British Adoption and Fostering Agencies, 1976.

21 Seglow, J., Pringle, M.K. and Wedge, P., *Growing up Adopted*, National Foundation for Education Research, 1972.

22 Grow, L.J. and Shapiro, D., *op.cit.*

23 Fanshel, D., *op.cit.*

24 Bagley, C. and Young, L., 'The identity, adjustment and achievement of transracially-adopted children: a review and empirical report' in Verma, G.K. and Bagley, C. (eds.), *Race, Education and Identity*, Macmillan, 1979.

25 Raynor, L., *op.cit.*, p. 172.

Chapter 2

1 Kitwood, T., *Disclosures to a Stranger*, Routledge and Kegan Paul, 1980, p. 6.

2 *ibid.*, p. 47.

3 Brah, A., Fuller, M., Louden, D. and Miles, R., 'Experimenter effects and the ethnic cueing phenomena', *SSRC working papers on ethnic relations*, no. 3.

4 See: Wilson, A., 'Mixed-race children: an exploratory study of racial categorization and identity', *New Community*, Spring – Summer 1981, pp. 36–43.

5 When reading this study it should be remembered that not only were we talking to the families and children at a particular time in their development, but we were interviewing at a particular time in the history of 'race relations' in this country: December 1980 to March 1981. Tensions related to race were apparently on the increase and certainly were gaining media attention. The Nationality Bill was being debated amidst renewed scapegoating in some quarters of the black community for the economic ills of the country. Major urban conflict related in part to the disadvantaged position of ethnic minorities had begun with the St Paul's riots of April 1980, and racist attacks had apparently doubled in the year 1980–1981. (See report compiled by Dr Zaka Khan, General Secretary to the Union of Pakistani Organisations of the UK and Europe, presented to the Home Office in July 1981. Reported in *The Observer*, 14 June, 1981).

Chapter 3

1 In two cases, the separated parents came together for the purpose of the research interview for the present study. In the other two, only the parent currently caring for the child was seen.

2 This figure includes all rooms in the household which are 'lived in'. Kitchens are included if 'lived in'. Toilets and bathrooms are excluded.

3 This is the definition of overcrowding used in the National Child Development study. See, for instance, Lambert, L. and Streather, J., *Children in Changing Families*, Macmillan, 1980, pp. 80–3.

Chapter 4

1 Kitwood, T., *op.cit.*, p. 122.

2 Raynor, L., *The Adopted Child Comes of Age*, George Allen and Unwin, 1980, p. 47.
3 *ibid.*, p. 104.
4 See, for instance, Jaffee, B. and Fanshel, D., *How They Fared in Adoption*, Columbia University Press, 1970.

Chapter 6

1 Parent to Parent Information about Adoption Services, *A PPIAS View of the Adoption of Black Children* (mimeo.), 1981.
2 Chestang, L., *op.cit.*
3 Samuels, A., *op.cit.*
4 Berger, P.L. and Luckman, T., *The Social Construction of Reality*, Allen Lane, The Penguin Press, 1967.

Chapter 7

1 Weinrich, P., 'Identity Development and Ethnicity: extension of personal construct theory'. Paper presented at second International Congress on Personal Construct Theory, Christ Church, Oxford, 1977.
2 Wilson, A., *op.cit.*, p. 41.
3 *ibid.*, p. 47. Wilson also notes the absence of the term 'black' in the vocabulary of her sample.
4 Douvan and Adelson note: 'The normal adolescent holds, we think, two conceptions of himself, what he is and what he will be — and the way in which he integrates the future image into his current life will indicate a good deal about his current adolescent integration'. Douvan, E. and Adelson, J., *The Adolescent Experience*, John Wiley, 1966. Quoted in Coleman, J., *The Nature of Adolescence*, Methuen, 1980.

Chapter 8

1 Coopersmith, S., *The Antecedents of Self-Esteem*, Freeman, San Francisco, 1967.
2 Holbrook, D., *Knowledge of Origins: self-esteem and family ties of long-term fostered and adopted children*; Department of Child and Adolescent Psychiatry, Institute of Psychiatry, London. This research is as yet unpublished. We are very grateful to Daphne Holbrook for permission to refer to this study and for the help which she gave us in comparing her results with our own.
3 'That the self-esteem of an individual remains constant for at least several years is demonstrated by measurements obtained under similar conditions and with relatively similar instruments. The test re-test reliability obtained for the self-esteem inventory after a five-week interval with a sample of 30 fifth-grade children was 88, and the reliability after a three-year interval with a different sample of 56 children was 70. This would suggest that at some time preceding middle childhood the individual arrives at a general appraisal of his worth, which remains relatively stable and enduring over a period of several years'. Coopersmith, S., *op.cit.*, p. 5.
Other studies have also indicated the stability of the self-concept in this period.

See, for instance, Engel, M., 'The stability of the self-concept in adolescence', *Journal of Abnormal and Social Psychiatry*, 1959, Vol. 58, pp. 211-15.

4 Rosenberg, M., *Society and the Adolescent Self-Image*, Princeton University Press, 1965.

5 Louden, M., *A comparative study of self-concept, self-esteem and locus of control in minority group adolescents in English multi-racial schools*. Unpublished Ph.D. thesis, University of Bristol, 1977.

6 Two items were discarded from the original scale by Louden ('I certainly feel useless at times' and 'All in all, I am inclined to think I am a failure'). These were replaced by two others ('I'don't care what happens to me' and 'Things are all mixed up in my life'). Following our pilot interviews, two further statements were discarded because, although the older children seemed able to respond readily and easily to them, some of the younger ones did not: 'I take a positive attitude towards myself' and 'I wish I could have more respect for myself'. It seemed that the words, and perhaps the concepts, involved in these two statements were too adult for some of the younger children in our study. We also had difficulty with 'I feel that I am a person of worth at least on an equal plane with others'. The children we talked to could not understand the idea of being on 'an equal plane' and so this statement was changed to 'I am a person at least equal with others'.

7 On the use of these scales see, for instance, Rutter, M., Tizard, J. and Whitmore, K. (eds.), *Education, Health and Behaviour*, Longman, 1970; and Rutter, M. *et al.*, 'Attainment and adjustment in two geographical areas: the prevalence of psychiatric disorder', *British Journal of Psychiatry*, no. 126, 1975, pp. 493-509.

8 As discussed in Chapter 3, the teachers of 32 of the children completed the questionnaire and the Rutter B scale.

9 Erikson, E., *Identity, Youth and Crisis*, Faber, 1968, pp. 168-9.

Chapter 9

1 See, for instance: Stack, C.B., *All our Kin: strategies for survival in a black community*, Harper and Row, 1974.

2 Chestang, L., *op.cit.*, pp. 103-4.

3 James, M., *op.cit.*, pp. 15-16.

4 Kitwood, T., *op.cit.*

Chapter 10

1 Sarosky, A.D., *The Adoption Triangle*, Nelson Doubleday Inc., Garden City, New York, 1979.

2 This speculation owes much to the work of Daphne Holbrook, who asked the parents and children she interviewed who initiated conversations and then compared the responses. See Holbrook, D., *op.cit.*

Chapter 12

1 Kadushin, A., *Adopting Older Children*, Columbia University Press, New York,

145

1970. Quoted in Simon, R.J. and Altstein, H., *op.cit.*, 1981.

2 Mandell, B.R., *Where are the Children? A class analysis of foster care and adoption*, Lexington Books, 1973, p. 3.

3 Holman, B., *Community Care*, 26 April 1978, p. 13.

4 ABAFA, *op.cit.*

5 See: 'Wanted — black families for black children', *Community Care*, 8 October 1981, and James, M., *op.cit.*

Select Bibliography

Articles

BAGLEY, C. and YOUNG, L., 'The identity, adjustment and achievement of transracially-adopted children: a review and empirical report', in VERMA, G.K. and BAGLEY, C. (eds.), *Race, Education and Identity*, Macmillan, 1979.

CHESTANG, L., 'The dilemma of biracial adoption', *Social Work* (USA), May 1972, pp. 100–101.

CHIMEZIE, A., 'Bold but irrelevant: Grow and Shapiro on transracial adoption', *Child Welfare*, vol. 56, February 1977, pp. 75–86.

FITZGERALD, J., 'Black parents for black children', *Adoption and Fostering*, no. 103, 1981, p. 10.

JACKSON, B., 'Inter-racial adoption' in WOLKIND, S. (ed.), *Medical Aspects of Adoption and Fostering*, Spastics International Medical Publications, 1979.

JAMES, M., 'Finding the families', *Adoption and Fostering*, no. 103, 1981, p. 12.

JONES, E.D., 'On transracial adoption of black children', *Child Welfare*, 51(3), 1972, pp. 156-164.

SAMUELS, A., 'Transracial adoption: adoption of the black child', *Family Law*, vol. 9, no. 8, 1979, p. 238.

Books and Pamphlets

ASSOCIATION OF BRITISH ADOPTION AND FOSTERING AGENCIES, *The Soul Kids Campaign*, ABAFA, 1976.

BENET, M.K., *The Character of Adoption*, Jonathan Cape, 1976.

DAY, D., *The Adoption of Black Children*, D.C. Heath, 1979.

FANSHEL, D., *Far from the Reservation: the transracial adoption of American Indian children*, Scarecrow Press, 1972.

GROW, L.C. and SHAPIRO, D., *Black Children, White Parents: a study of transracial adoption*, Child Welfare League of America, 1974.

JACKSON, B., *Family Experience of Inter-racial Adoption*, Association of British Adoption and Fostering Agencies, 1976.

JACKSON, B., *Adopting a Black Child*, Association of British Adoption and Fostering Agencies, 1976.

RAYNOR, L., *Adoption of Non-White Children in Britain*, Allen and Unwin, 1970.

SIMON, R.J. and ALTSTEIN, H., *Transracial Adoption*, John Wiley, 1977.

SIMON, R.J. and ALTSTEIN, H., *Transracial Adoption: a follow-up*, Lexington Books, 1981.

INDEX